Feeding the Family

100 Years of Food and Drink in Victoria

Feeding the Family
100 Years of Food and Drink in Victoria

Nancy Oke & Robert Griffin

ROYAL **BC** MUSEUM
Victoria, Canada

Published by the Royal BC Museum, 675 Belleville Street, Victoria, British Columbia, V8W 9W2, Canada.

Printed in Canada.

Front-cover photograph: John Ward's grocery store at 1728 Quadra Street, 1910. Courtesy of Nancy Oke.

Back-cover photograph: See page 21 for details.

See page 155 for more information on copyright, permissions and credits.

Library and Archives Canada Cataloguing in Publication

Oke, Nancy, 1930-
    Feeding the family : 100 years of food and drink in Victoria / Nancy Oke & Robert Griffin.

    Includes bibliographical references and index.
    ISBN 978-0-7726-6343-6

    1. Food – British Columbia – Victoria – History.
2. Food industry and trade – British Columbia – Victoria – History. 3. Victoria (B.C.) – History.
I. Griffin, Robert Brian, 1951– II. Royal BC Museum.
III. Title.

TX360.C33V53 2011   641.3'00971128   2011-902627-9

MIX
Paper from responsible sources
FSC® C103113
www.fsc.org

Contents

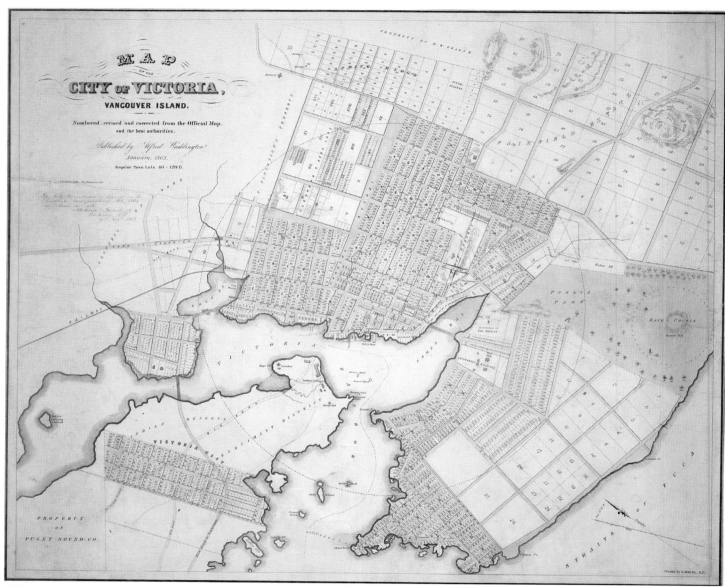

Alfred Waddington's 1863 map shows a growing city. Most of the lots away from the town centre are vacant, though a few hardy settlers lived as far out of town as Quadra Street. A few homes on Vancouver and Cook streets began to appear by 1867. Spring Ridge, Victoria's main source water at this time, is at the end of Pandora Avenue, in the upper centre of the map. BC Archives CM B272.

Introduction

During the last half of the 19th century, Victoria was the commercial powerhouse of British Columbia. Victoria's merchants owned fish canneries on the Skeena, financed cattle ranches in the province's interior and supplied the goldfields with their goods. As the largest city in British Columbia, Victoria was also the largest market. Businesses flourished and died here, and they were essential to the rest of the province. The commission agents and wholesalers who brought in goods for Victoria also supplied much of BC.

When Canadian Pacific Railway arrived on the west coast in 1886, and when Vancouver was chosen as its main Pacific terminal, Victoria's dominance ended and a new era began for British Columbia. Some of Victoria's wholesalers closed shop in the face of Vancouver's advantages. Others, such as Robert Rithet, decided to remain in Victoria, but their roles in the province's economy declined as the 20th century progressed. Now the leading wholesale merchants for groceries were Kelly Douglas and WH Malkin, both with headquarters in Vancouver. Victoria's retailers still plied their trade, although no longer in the province's largest population centre and only a few vestiges of Victoria's past glory remained – Ormonds still produced its widely recognized biscuits and Rithet's wharf-side warehouses continued to be filled with goods.

The sources of Victoria's food also changed through the colonial period, the late 19th century and the 20th century. More food arrived and in ever greater variety, but at the expense of local production; biscuit manufacturers disappeared, and local packing and food preparation establishments changed hands and finally closed. How food was handled and packaged also changed dramatically: fresh peas available in season became tinned peas and eventually frozen peas available all year round. The new technologies also changed the way consumers purchased food: they no longer shopped daily at groceries, bakeries, butcher shops and fish mongers', because they could now store their food for days or even weeks. Canning, freezing and household appliances, such as the refrigerator and electric stove, profoundly changed our buying and eating habits.

Retail changes significantly altered the look of Victoria streets as the small shops yielded to larger shops and finally to self-service supermarkets. Victoria did not completely follow the pattern of most emerging communities that developed a dependence on general stores and markets. Victoria never established a successful public market, and specialty shops continued to dominate the retail trade. In keeping with the national trend, however, Victoria's specialized bakers, butchers and grocers eventually gave way to general food stores like

Fort Victoria, 1854. Unknown artist; BC Archives A-04104.

Kirkham's and Batchlor's. The specialty stores still existed, but not in the numbers of earlier decades. The major change came in the 1920s with the arrival of the large chain self-serve stores, like Piggly Wiggly and Safeway, which began to edge out the locally-owned retailers. The large department stores such as Spencer's, Woodward's and the Hudson's Bay Company also expanded their food floors, creating centralized buying options for the consumer. Customers no longer stood at the counter while store clerks gathered the goods on their shopping list from a limited range of products. The self-serve outlets began to provide a broader choice for each product – now a customer could choose from several brands of canned peas, not just one or two.

Victoria was, from its founding, an importer of foods. When the population mushroomed in 1858,

goods began to arrive from many exotic places; oranges and other fruits appeared, as well as specialty products from other countries. Many of the goods only available in today's specialty shops were then locally made and standard fare on Victoria's larger food-store shelves. The biscuits you ate were probably made in Victoria, as was the jam; your coffee or tea may have been packed locally and the flour ground locally. Vinegar, salad dressing and all sorts of other goods were produced locally and sold to Victorians.

As the 19th century progressed, change here also appeared. A wider variety of goods meant greater competition, and eventually many of the small manufacturers gave way to national and international producers. A small biscuit manufacturer producing limited quantities could not compete

Victoria Harbour, 1880s. BC Archives A-00176.

with a large eastern-Canadian manufacturer baking and packaging thousands of biscuits a day. While the consumer was now sometimes presented with a wider choice, they were limited in other ways, for almost no packaged foods were produced locally.

As these many changes took place, Victoria itself changed in status and stature. To some extent, the 19th and 20th centuries represented very different eras for the provincial capital. In the 19th century Victoria was the leading city in BC; in the 20th century Vancouver took over this position. In the 19th century small retailers dominated commerce in Victoria; in the 20th century big grocery chains moved in and gradually dominated the retail trade. The wholesale trade changed, too, from the early multitude of small commission agents to fewer, much larger importers of goods.

Still, the Victoria story is unique, because the players' disctinct characteristics provide vivid examples of just how unpredictable life can be.

PIGGLY WIGGLY

FOODS YOU KNOW at the Lowest Prices in Years

ROBINSON'S
Cut Mixed **PEEL**
½ Lb., 10c; 1 Lb. ___ 19c

B.C. POOL GUARANTEED FRESH
EGGS
Extras, Dozen _____ **60c**

SQUIRREL
Peanut Butter
No. 1 Tin, 18c

CANADIAN
Macaroni
3 Large 16-oz. Packages ____ **25c**

KRAFT'S
NUKRAFT, Pkt. ____ 20c
Ontario Cream Cheese, Lb., 25c

ROYAL CROWN
Sal Soda or Ammonia ... **2** pks. **13c**

BUTTER
SUNSET GOLD
3 1-lb. Cartons ____ **$1.10**
CHOICE CREAMERY
3 1-lb. Prints **$1.05**

● The rapid turnover of PIGGLY WIGGLY stocks make it possible to pass to our customers—IMMEDIATELY—the benefits of lower market prices, as well as giving you the finest in Fresh, Clean Foods.

FRIDAY AND SATURDAY

Aylmer Choice PEAS, Sieve 5, 3 Tins	25c
Gold Medal MAYONNAISE, 8-Oz. Jar	25c
Little Chip MARMALADE, 12-Oz. Jar	19c
Empress Pure Black Currant JAM, 4-Lb.	59c
B.C. TOMATOES, Large 2½ Tin	10c
Colman's MUSTARD, 4-Oz., 25c; 8-Oz.	49c

1 lb. Braid's Blue Label TEA
And Decorated China Cup and Saucer—All for **42c**

NEW CROP WALNUTS Shelled Halves—lb. ... 37c / Shelled Quarters—lb. ... 33c

Bleached Seedless RAISINS Fancy Quality	2 Lbs., 27c
ROMAN MEAL, Package	31c
Robin Hood OATS, Large Package	19c
Princess SOAP FLAKES (1 Large, 1 Small)	19c
MATCHES, Owl, 300's, Made in Canada	3 Pks., 25c
LUX, Small, 3 for 25; Large, Packet	20c

FRESH FRUITS AND VEGETABLES
ORANGES, Sunkist Navels, good size, 2 dozen	49¢
LEMONS, Sunkist, 2 dozen	23¢
GRAPES, finest quality, 2 lbs.	19¢
POTATOES, finest quality Netted Gems, 10 lbs. in handy Shopping Bag	19¢
CARROTS, local grown, bunches; 3 bunches	5¢

SHOP THE MODERN ECONOMICAL WAY

Ad in the *Colonist* on November 21, 1930.

Gardens and Farms

"About ½ acre land delved in the Garden."
 – Fort Victoria Post Journal, April 1847.

The "delving" of the land began as soon as Fort Victoria was established in 1843. James Douglas ordered his Hudson's Bay Company employees to clear and plough land so that gardens could be planted. He hoped that the fort would be self-sufficient, but he also knew that growing conditions at Fort Victoria were not as favourable as those at Fort Vancouver. In a letter written in 1850, Douglas contrasted the soil in Victoria with that on the Columbia River. Vancouver Island, he noted, was a place of "rocky ridges, stony land and bushy glades", while the land at Fort Vancouver encompassed "extensive prairies without a bush or stone to check the progress of the plough" (Fort Victoria Correspondence). Company officials in London had trouble understanding these conditions, many being familiar only with the arable fields of Britain.

The work at Victoria began with the clearing of fields and the planting of grain crops. The local natives made up most of the labour force, with up to 100 indigenous workers clearing the brush and trees. Company workers established gardens for fruit and vegetables. They planted wheat, oats and barley on the plains around the fort, and wheat and timothy among trees; wild poppies grew among the cereal grasses. At harvest time, women and children helped to sort and store the crops. On the north side of Fort Street stood one of the Hudson's Bay Company's barns, its clapboard sides covered with large pieces of cedar bark, and more company barns lined Fort Street to Blanshard.

Once the planting was done a successful crop depended on the weather. HBC personnel did not fully understand growing conditions on the island and they noted many failures in the fort report. Potatoes planted in the shade of Garry Oaks failed to produce. Dry seasons forced crops to be planted late, only to be destroyed by early frosts. In 1848, measles sickened two-thirds of the fort's population, including most of the Hawaiian labourers who worked the fields, and the company struggled to bring in the crop that year. In 1851, in his first year as governor of the colony of Vancouver Island, James Douglas reported that the countryside around Fort Victoria was not suited to the large farms envisioned by the Hudson's Bay Company.

We have taken up our potatoes … only 850 bushels.… The oak trees being left in the field did them considerable injury, few or none having grown in their shade.… We are therefore having them down.
 – Letter from Roderick Finlayson at Fort Victoria to Chief Factor John McLaughlin in Fort Vancouver, October 10, 1844.

Fort Victoria and the Hudson's Bay Company garden, about 1858. When it came to be sold, the company listed the garden as 2300 by 200 feet (700 x 60 m). Henry Crease sketch (attributed). BC Archives B-08622.

Granny always bought venison, fish, ducks and berries from the Songhees Indians who landed their canoes at the bottom of the garden. The food would be distributed to the poor and the Indians sent away loaded up with fruit and vegetables from the garden.
– Colonel James Harris, grandson of Amelia Douglas (from *Victoria: The Way It Was* by Michael Kluckner).

On March 23, 1849, Dr William Tolmie at Fort Nisqually wrote to Roderick Finlayson, chief factor at Fort Victoria, saying, "A very valuable package of garden and agricultural seeds have been sent me. I beg you open – and to take a share of the seeds for Victoria." Seeds were also sent from Fort Vancouver, as were small fruit trees. Others seeds and small trees came from other locations in the Territory of Oregon. Seeds were an important resource – in 1851 Governor Douglas wrote a letter to Archibald Barkley, the HBC's secretary in London, England, carefully explaining how they should be shipped and handled. He warned that the seeds must be checked to ensure that they were not mixed with inferior or damaged seeds, then packed in bags and stored in tightly sealed barrels. The seeds, he said, should be "frequently aired in fine weather only by a careful person" during the voyage and "we entreat that the seeds may be fresh and of the best kinds".

Seeds for gardens and HBC lands were soon being shipped directly from England, enabling the colonists to plant what they were familiar with from the Old Country. Fresh Vancouver Island seeds also became available each year, guaranteed to be satisfactory. The arrival of the gold miners in 1858 and the support services that accompanied them greatly expanded the available supplies of seeds and plants. As more and more people settled in the town, some started home gardens. The druggists of the town offered packets of seeds for sale. In 1858 Jay & Company started a nursery business at 5 Fort Street, and operated a field for nursery stock at Cook and Pandora streets. Packets of seeds sold for 12½ cents each and up. In the *Colonist* newspaper, Jay & Company advertised two-year-old fruit trees for sale at 15 cents each and four-year-old trees at 25 cents

Tsartlip Indian Huts Outside the Governor's Garden, October 1860. Sarah Crease painting. BC Archives PDP02899.

They have cleared a quantity of ground, and have some acres of wheat besides vegetables.... The people are kept up late, as it is harvest time, and they dare not cut the wheat away in the day, it being so dry that all the grains fall out, so they wait until a little dew has fallen and then go on working until past 12 at night.
  – Letter from an officer on HMS *Constant* to Henry Labouchere, August 16, 1848.

each. In 1864 the company advertised seeds for a large garden at $5, a medium garden for $3.50, and a small garden for $3.00. One dollar could also buy 100 British Queen strawberry plants from Henry Henley at Clover Point.

The Hudson's Bay Company planted vegetables in a six-acre (2.4-hectare) garden bounded by today's Government, Fort, Broad and Broughton streets. A fence made of logs brought in canoes by the natives surrounded the garden, though later correspondence described it as a white picket fence. On October 10, 1844, only a year after the fort was established, its chief factor, Roderick Finlayson, reported that medical men from HMS *Cadboro* had come ashore for a visit and "after having been supplied with vegetables from our Garden … embarked". The HBC planted a great quantity of potatoes in the fields around the fort and reported the yield in detail annually.

HBC employees planted the fort's first orchard in 1846 in the company garden at the corner of Fort and Government streets, beginning with transplanted apple trees. Pioneers reminiscing about Fort Victoria's early days often mention that fruit was in short supply, and that, sometimes, the HBC barque *Columbia* would bring a luxury such as an apple from Fort Vancouver for Amelia Douglas, the governor's wife. Edgar Fawcett remembered that as a young boy he stole apples from the company gardens in the early 1850s. Soon, a grape vine and small soft fruits joined the apple trees in the garden.

In 1860 the HBC sold the garden for $12,000 to Leopold Loewenberg, who divided the land into small lots and offered them for sale. Some of the lots became a public market in 1861 (see page 129), and later James Fell's grocery and Moses Rowe Smith's bakery were built on the site (pages 25 and 61).

On a small plot of land on the edge of the south end of the fort, Reverend Robert Staines established a garden that would become well known for excellent gooseberries and its lettuce, a welcome highlight at evening supper. There is a story that someone mistakenly dressed a dinner salad with castor oil, causing Staines's overnight guests great distress. Reverend Staines expected his students to work in the garden thinning and weeding, an occupation one described as miserable. Yet the students themselves had a small garden adjacent to the fort where James Anderson, an early settler, remembered, they "played" at gardening.

Potatoes became the most common vegetable eaten by the colonists. In 1842, when James Douglas first came to the site where Fort Victoria would be built, he found the native people already growing potatoes. First Peoples seem to have adopted the potato at least a decade prior to the establishment of Fort Victoria; they may have obtained them from Fort Langley or Fort Nisqually. Turnips and carrots also seem to have quickly become part of the standard fare of local First Peoples. Some colonists described the native planting technique as simply burying the seed under the green turf and moving to another area when the ground proved less fertile. Local natives sold a backload of potatoes for one shilling, and the colonists considered them excellent quality. The Hudson's Bay Company also traded for potatoes with the Cowichan to the north.

As Victoria grew, so did the pressure to produce enough food for the settlers and the crews of incoming ships. In 1844, John McLaughlin, chief factor for the Columbia District, instructed Roderick Finlayson to "continue extending your fields as far as the means at your disposal permit, as Fort Victoria will soon be expected to furnish a large quantity of grain".

Potato Yield

1846	2100 bushels
1847	3000 bushels
1848	3000 bushels

A bushel of potatoes weighs about 50 lb or 23 kg. The daily potato ration for a labourer in 1850 was two pounds.

The mission must have seemed daunting. Douglas, for his part, thought that settlers should not be sent to Vancouver Island, because the place had "too much precipitation", which could lead to food shortages. He suggested that 100 people, men, women and children, were the optimum for each of two years. "Afterwards," he wrote, "the numbers should be in proportion to our means of producing food." But Victoria was soon inundated with hordes of men heading to the gold fields, while HBC ships brought more permanent settlers. Douglas's plan for a slow colonization and a self-sufficient settlement was clearly not to be, and large quantities of produce would need to be imported.

The future of farming and gardening did not seem too promising to the new colonists of 1858. In his book, *The Fraser Mines Vindicated*, published that year, Alfred Waddington declared the land to be a poor apology for an agricultural country: "The whole country would not make a fair-sized milk ranch in California." On the other hand, an editorial in the *Colonist* on July 3, 1858, titled "Hints to the Enterprising", suggested that gardeners "could in a few months be engaged in an extremely profitable business in the raising of vegetables, which are even scarcer now than they were in San Francisco in 1849". It was all in the way you looked at it.

The new settlers began to grow their own vegetables and fruits in small gardens. These home gardens kept fruits and vegetables on the table. Emily Carr, in *The Book of Small*, remembers the garden at her family home:

> We had an orchard and a great tin-lined apple room, wonderful strawberry beds and raspberry and currant bushes, all imported English stock, and an Isabella grape vine…. We had chickens and cows and a pig, a grand vegetable

Anton Henderson and family at their vegetable garden on
Rupert Street, Victoria, about 1890. BC Archives G-03868.

garden – almost everything we ate grew on our
own place.

Many home gardens became mini-farms. Cows,
horses, pigs, and poultry all found their place among
the fruits and vegetables, and the settlers built small
barns near their houses. Excess produce could always
be sold to someone in the town, and often the grocer
would add them to his stock.

The owners of these small gardens often
reported damage done by crop-eating pigs, maraud-
ing cows and poultry-killing dogs. On July 24, 1869,
a letter writer in the *Colonist* contended that people

whose dogs carried out such depredations "need
not feel aggrieved if they (the dogs) are summarily
disposed of by those whose premises they frequently
invade". People also took liberties in home gardens:
a group of apple thieves brazenly attempted to sell
stolen apples to the person who apprehended them
in the orchard.

The O'Reilly family left careful notes about the
plantings in their vegetable gardens at Point Ellice
House. The kitchen garden was to the south of the
house. It supplied a wide variety of vegetables. The
O'Reillys planted broad beans, beets, cabbage, celery,

Vegetables arrived in Victoria from many locations.
BC Archives H-01141.

Willie Pottinger, 1880s. He worked for
the Hudson's Bay Company before
becoming the gardener at Hillside
Farm. Richard Maynard photograph;
BC Archives I-51746.

horseradish, lettuce, onions, parsley, peas, radishes,
scarlet runner beans, turnips and other vegetables. In
1858, the family notes mention rampion, a popular
root vegetable at that time, much like parsnip; but
they point out rampion's weedy and invasive habit.
Salsify was another popular root vegetable. Seeds for
all these vegetables could be obtained from the local
chemist shop or ordered from England. The O'Reillys
also planted fruit trees and bushes, listing in their
records cherry, apple, currant, filbert and mulberry.
Later records extended the list of plantings to all
vegetables commonly available today. The family
also grew vetch and mungold (a type of beet) for
animal feed.

On Clover Point, with its sweeping view of
Juan de Fuca Strait, Henry Henley established his
hotel and market garden. He grew a wide variety
of vegetables for sale, and sold seeds and plants to
the local home gardeners; he also advertised that
he would lay out gardens and keep them in order

for the season. Henley boasted about his cabbages
– he advertised that he had six varieties, and one
ad in the *Victoria Press* (October 12, 1861) said that
he had "two hundred thousand plants of eight
varieties" for sale. On October 3, 1863, the *Victoria
Chronicle* described his entry of a model farm in the
Agricultural and Horticultural Society Exhibition as
"complete in every detail with numerous plants and
vegetables – among the latter, six varieties of cabbage". Having used what produce he needed in the
hotel dining room, Henley delivered vegetables and
fruit into town by cart. His main challenger in the
contest to grow extra-large fruits and vegetables was
possibly Willie Pottinger (also know as Old Willie),
the gardener at Hillside Farm near Quadra Street
and Queens Avenue. Pottinger's prize effort was a
60-pound cabbage. His strawberries also drew strong
praise in the *Victoria Press* (June 9, 1862) as "the finest
fruit that has ever made its appearance at this time in
Victoria … the smallest of the strawberries is about

A woman shows off the vegetables in her home garden, 1913. BC Archives C-02241.

Chinese vegetable seller. BC Archives I-63406.

4 inches [10 cm] in circumference". Other home gardeners were just as eager to promote their large fruits and vegetables, a source of great pride for the grower. Their efforts were exhibited in many merchants' windows and described vividly in the "Local News" column of the *Colonist*. From these notes the townspeople heard of 27-pound beets, 65-pound turnips, 2½-pound onions and other monster specimens.

During the First World War, home gardens became an essential part of the war effort as food shortages took hold. The City Council engaged in an active campaign to encourage the full use of vacant lots and backyards for the production of food.

By 1921, a few years after the war ended, the city council expressed its concern In its annual report) that the land being used for home gardens was not being put to the best use:

> Vacant lot cultivation is carried on not by those who really should do so to provide vegetables for their families during the winter months, but by persons who make this form of production a pastime and in many cases giving the produce to others who will not help themselves by cultivating a vacant lot.

The gardens tilled by the Chinese, and on which many households depended for their fresh vegeta-

The Home for the Aged in Victoria, about 1892. BC Archives I-63406.

bles to be delivered door-to-door, did not receive the same high praise afforded the townspeople's home gardens. Anti-Chinese sentiment ran high at this time and writers in the *Colonist* (July 17, 1891) described Chinese vegetables as "typhoid breeding", because they came from gardens fertilized with night soil, human waste "manufactured into a liquid guano" whose "disagreeable odours sickened the people residing contiguous to the nuisance". ("Night soil" is still used as fertilizer in some parts of the world.)

Editorials in the newspaper repeated the theme that the "Chinese Must Go" and expressed particularly virulent anti-Chinese opinions, yet people had to admit that prior to the arrival of the Chinese and their widespread participation in gardening, vegetables were in short supply. Many Chinese gardens were along Queens Avenue and the surrounding streets. Others were located on Cedar Hill Road, and still others in Spring Ridge, and at the end of Cook Street. In *The Book of Small*, Emily Carr described the "patient blue-jean figures" that worked in their gardens, carrying water in five-gallon (23-litre) cans balanced on poles across their backs and watering each plant individually.

Institutions such as the jail and the hospital frequently operated with limited public funds, making the economic feeding of the inmates and residents of great concern. In 1863 it was estimated that it cost 63 cents a day to feed an inmate in the jail. Fresh produce was best supplied by growing fruits and vegetables in an adjacent garden and supplementing them with produce from a local merchant who was contracted to supply them at a fixed price.

The garden at the Home for the Aged was maintained by the men themselves, as much as they were physically able. Each year the home sought to feed the men and keep the cost to the city as low as possible, reporting in great detail their successes and failures. The need to purchase vegetables was taken as a sign of defeat, but purchase them they did when the crops were not as good as expected. The home was located near the Ross Bay Cemetery and some of the cemetery land was used for the garden, although in 1901 it was noted that the ground was too sour and poor and very unsuitable for raising vegetables. Later, some of this cemetery land was traded for a plot of land considered more suitable.

Gradually the garden expanded. The Home for

Planting potatoes, Southgate Street, early 1920s. Victoria
City Archives 98303-07-386.

the Aged bought pigs and then sold them for a profit.
The City of Victoria's annual report recounted the
garden's progress. In 1895, the men laid a water pipe
and purchased a rubber hose "to secure a plentiful
supply of water conveniently". In 1898 the crop was
so abundant that they were even able to share some
of the produce with the Home for Aged Women. The
year 1919 must have been particularly gratifying,
because "no tender was called for vegetables, the
garden supplying all required for the year, and great
credit is due Mr Brown, the gardener". But such
successes were rare. Some seasons the gardeners
pleaded for manure. The city's 1905 annual report
described a plague of cut worms "creating great

havoc among the cabbages", reducing 500 plants to
just 17 heads. The garden's greatest strength was
its production of potatoes. When all else failed, the
potato crop always came through.

When the Royal Hospital moved to its present
location at Fort and Richmond streets in 1890, it hired
a gardener at $30 a month to start a large garden.
"The Farm", as it was referred to, grew vegetables
and raised animals to provide patients with fresh
produce and milk. The gardener dug a well to defray
the heavy expense of water delivered by cart. The
hospital kept careful accounts and sought extra
produce when the garden did not supply enough for
its needs. The Farm continued operating until 1925.

Picnic party at Craigflower Farm, 1865. BC Archives A-01441.
>The farm was beautifully laid out, bounded by the Gorge Arm on one side and the garden sloped to the front of it.
>
>– Martha (Douglas) Harris.

As soon as the Sisters of St Ann arrived in Victoria in 1853, they began a small garden, according to archivist Margaret Cantwell. As their base the sisters used an orchard already established by Leon Morel, a servant of the Hudson's Bay Company, from whom Bishop Demers had acquired a squared-timber house and some surrounding land. As more land was obtained and the convent community grew, the gardens came under the care of individual sisters. Vegetables and fruits of all kinds thrived at the convent. In 1912, a city ordinance restricted animals on city lots. In that same year the Sisters began Providence Farm near Duncan. The land around the Victoria convent continued to be developed as a fruit and vegetable garden. Since restoration of St Ann's Academy began in 1995, some of the early fruit trees have been refurbished.

Home gardens and institutional gardens were small in comparison to the lands under cultivation at farms. The Hudson's Bay Company established three farms in the 1840s: Beckley Farm in James Bay supplied the fort with vegetables; farther east, Uplands Farm raised much of the company's livestock; and North Dairy Farm to the north. Additional farms were also established, usually by company employ-ees and retirees. One of these men was John Work of Hillside Farm, who thought that farming was "rather uphill work, yielding little, if any, profit". But Martha Douglas considered Hillside Farm "a true Bible place, filled with rich land and running streams and springs [where] the garden was so large and vegetables grew in abundance". The three HBC farms were the main suppliers of meat and produce until the 1850s, when the company brought more agricultural land under production through the Puget Sound Agricultural Company (PSAC).

A subsidiary of the Hudson's Bay Company, PSAC operated farms near Fort Vancouver and Fort Nisqually. These farms also helped supply Fort Victoria until the HBC decided to extend its holdings to Vancouver Island. PSAC brought into production four farms near Victoria beginning in 1851, the first occupying 1,042 hectares that stretched from town out through Esquimalt. A bailiff managed each of the four properties: Viewfield, Colwood, Constance Cove and Craigflower farms. Of the 245 hectares at Viewfield, only 15 were under cultivation by 1855. Craigflower was the most successful operation, with a flour mill and a substantial bakery. By 1856 there were enough settlers in the area for a public market

The garden on the grounds of St Ann's Convent on
Heywood Avenue. BC Archives C-05380.

Berry pickers.
Victoria City Archives 98303-07-380.

to be held at the farm each month. All these farms required labourers – about 15 seemed to work on each property – and they were hired mainly from the native population who each received two blankets a month and their rations.

Private farms were gradually established as settlers arrived and more servants left the employ of the HBC. The districts of Saanich, Esquimalt, Sooke and Metchosin saw the spread of settlers. Transportation of the produce along the rutted roads to the Victoria markets was difficult, and many farmers took to the water and rowed their produce to town. By 1891 about 20 truck farms surrounded Victoria, varying in size from 1 to 20 acres (a half to eight hectares). The 1894 census reported just over 9000 acres (about 3700 hectares) in farmland, with half of that being in Saanich. The roads by this time had improved and a railway ran through the area, making access to Victoria much easier. By the 1890s much of the labour on these farms was provided by Asians, who were

paid at a much lower rate than the scarce Caucasian labourers. In 1903 Caucasians earned $20 to $30 per month, while the Chinese and the Japanese received about half of that wage. First Nations workers were paid about the same as the Chinese.

Despite all this effort put into growing gardens and cultivating farms, the amount of produce grown was insufficient to fully supply local needs and Victoria remained an importer of food.

Shelbourne Valley Farm, Saanich, with Mount Tolmie in
behind, 1880s. Hannah or Richard Maynard photograph;
BC Archives D-08697

Agricultural Wages in 1903
Reported in *Land and Agriculture in BC* (British Columbia government).

Place	European	Chinese	Japanese	First Nations
Colwood	$20–30/month	$10–30/month	$5–30/month	
Sooke	$1.50/day	$20/month	$10/month	
Cowichan		$1/day	$8–10/month*	men $2/day
				women $1/day
Gulf Islands	$1.50–2/day	$.50/day or $6–15/month*		

* with board

Durrance Farm, Saanich, 1880s. Richard or Hannah
Maynard photograph; BC Archives D-08709.

The Grocers

In 1858, a year before the Hudson's Bay Company announced that it would deal in wholesale only, Peter Lester and Mifflin Gibbs opened the first grocery and provision store in Victoria. The crowds of miners heading to the Fraser River needed supplies, as did the growing number of settlers – an opportunity not to be missed. The number of groceries quickly mushroomed. We know little about many of them, perhaps a small advertisement or a name in a directory. Advertisements heralded the establishment of new stores and auctioneers announced the demise of others. Some grocery stores became more prominent and it is these that we can look at today, through comments in the newspapers, their advertisements and surviving photographs of the stores, frequently with the owners standing proudly at the front door or behind the counter.

The city directory listed 20 groceries in 1860 and more than 30 in 1867. From these notices we can picture the stock-filled barrels and shelves filled with a range of local and imported foods. The grocery business was a risky one, however, and stores came and went, with only a few able to survive the vicissitudes of the commerce. Success was highest among those who had experience before coming to Victoria, and some even lasted into the 20th century, often managed by sons who inherited the business. Many of the owners of the small groceries did not survive financially and went on to other enterprises. Some chose to "skedaddle", taking their money and that of their partner with them. Others simply went out of business. In 1863, when Benrimo and White (later Benrimo and Denny), proprietors of a grocery store on Johnson Street near Government, decided they no longer wished to "execute orders and deliver with promptitude" as they had been doing for several years, they left the disposal of their stock to auctioneer J.A. McCrae. On March 21 he placed an ad in the *Colonist* listing, among other things, bacon, hams, pickles, pie fruits, cheeses, spices, teas, coffee and "a large quantity of potatoes and vegetables". The scales, counter and cooking stove also went on sale.

Commercial merchants along Wharf and Store streets also sold groceries. Shipments of preserved and fresh produce arrived with

I was so amused at your objection to your Gardener's Wife's Cousin calling on you! Here everybody calls on you. All the Shopkeepers call! Our Grocer apologized for his Wife not being well enough to see me!... And today I went to ask after her husband, who has been very ill, and she asked me into her "back Parlour" and shook hands &c &c.
– Mary Susanne Moody in a letter to her sister, about 1860.

J.D. Carroll's store at 6 Yates Street, about 1868. Carroll soon left the general-grocery trade to sell wine and liquor. Frederick Dally photograph; BC Archives A-03038.

each ship and were auctioned to the local retailers. Shipments from England brought a little bit of Old Country food preserved in tins and bottles. French products made up a share of the imports and proved very popular. From Hawaii came sugar, molasses and rice.

Peter Lester and Mifflin Gibbs were among the first merchants to challenge the Hudson's Bay Company's grocery monopoly. They were business partners in San Francisco before sailing to Victoria in June 1858. They brought with them miner's outfits that they sold on board the ship. On landing, Gibbs hastened to acquire property where he and Lester might set up shop. The *Daily Evening Bulletin*, a San Francisco newspaper published for the territories

of Oregon and Washington, quoted him saying that the business in Victoria was "generally run by old fogies" who were "destitute of Yankee enterprise".

On June 23, the *Bulletin* published a letter from Gibbs that expressed his regret in not having left for Victoria earlier. "If either of us had arrived here two months ago worth $1000, we could have been worth $10,000 today." Lester and Gibbs established a general store on the north side of Yates Street near Waddington Alley, almost opposite the new Wells Fargo office. From there they sold groceries, hardware, miner's outfits, Golden Gate flour, bacon, butter, Java and Rio coffees, black tea, crushed sugar, lobsters, oysters, Worcester sauce, lard, pickles and syrups, which arrived daily by ship. They advertised

Neufelder & Ross, grocery importers, on the east side of
Wharf Street, 1880s. BC Archives B-00510.

Right: W.B. Smith Groceries, 1862.
G.R. Fardon photograph; BC Archives D-07255.

Price of Butter per Pound	
1858	75¢
1859	50¢
1860	37½¢
1870	50¢
1880	25–30¢
1890	37½¢
1900	20¢

Peter Lester, 1858.
BC Archives A-01626.

Mifflin Westal Gibbs, about 1873.
BC Archives B-01661.

all their goods in detail and guaranteed to sell them at "low rates". Their advertisements remained unchanged over all the years they were in business. Their company was one of only a few that advertised in the short-lived French-language newspaper *Le Courier de la Nouvelle Caledonie*.

Lester and Gibbs did so well that the *Colonist* reported the grocers already making improvements to their store in 1859. In the early 1860s they expanded further, and Gibbs built an elaborate store, named Victoria House, on Government Street. The partnership dissolved in February 1864. Gibbs remained in the grocery business and engaged in other enterprises until he returned to the United States in 1869. Peter Lester stayed in Victoria and worked for several businesses.

Other grocers soon vied with Lester and Gibbs for a share in the business of providing "the best produce available" to their customers. C.P. Dart set

up shop in the Gazette Building on Yates Street in 1858, moving to Waddington Alley in 1860. Dart dealt in provisions, groceries and miners' tools. J.D. Carroll came from San Francisco to start a grocery and liquor store at 6 Yates Street. He quickly left the grocery trade to others, and concentrated on the more lucrative liquor and wine business, dealing in both wholesale and retail. Charles Bayley opened the Red House Grocery at 86-88 Yates as one of his many enterprises. Bayley's son, writing of his early days in Victoria, described the Red House Grocery as one of the first red brick buildings in Victoria at a time when the colony was a sea of tents. Bayley not only sold groceries to departing miners, but also ran a pack train to the gold mines at Leech River every Tuesday and Friday "freight or no freight".

Among those seeking "a share of the public patronage" was William Burlington Smith. He opened a store in 1858 on Government Street

P. Manetta & Company on Johnson Street, 1868.
BC Archives C-09033.

Lester and Gibbs' thriving business drew customers, but it also attracted thieves:

Robbery of a Shop Window: About 1 o'clock on Tuesday morning last, the shop window of Lester and Gibbs on Yates Street was broken into, and goods to the value of $10 stolen there from. The crashing of the window light awakened the party in charge of the store, but before he could get to the door, the robber or robbers made off with their plunder. This smashing operation should serve as a warning to shop keepers who are in the habit of allowing their goods to remain in their windows at night. They should protect them with strong shutters.
– *Weekly Victoria Gazette*,
  July 9, 1859.

Doing a Smashing Business:
Bayley of the Red House Grocery is selling off his stock for the purpose of closing his business. Business has not been very brisk lately and yesterday a horse belonging to an old settler, while hitched to a post of the veranda in front of the store, suddenly conceived the idea of helping the member for Nanaimo to dispose of some of his fixtures, so deliberately braced himself and tore down the whole veranda, which in its fall smashed the bow windows ... [with] damage about $70.
– *Victoria Chronicle*,
  September 12, 1863.

Typical invoices used by grocers in the late 19th and early 20th centuries.
RBCM 2000.33.38 and 2000.33.16.

Henry Saunders's grocery store, 1870s. BC Archives C-06376.

A man named Patrick Flynn was charged by [grocer] John Gennetson with stealing butter from his store. [Flynn] pleaded guilty and was sentenced to 3 months' imprisonment with hard labour.
– *Victoria Press*, April 16, 1861.

opposite the fort where he offered "a choice stock of Foreign and Domestic Groceries, Provisions, etc, selected with care and attention to this market" (*Victoria Gazette*, October 22, 1858). In 1868 he replaced what must have been a wooden building with one of brick on the same site. The advertisements he and fellow grocer Thomas Phelan placed in the newspaper stand out as the only ones featuring a small engraving as part of the design.

Like other merchants, Smith did not confine himself to supplying groceries and provisions. He offered storage space for the trunks that miners wished to leave behind before they headed up to the Cariboo. On returning to Victoria, they would find their belongings carefully stored in a booth with 1700 other trunks. The charge for this was one dollar a month, which miners frequently paid in gold dust. Some of these trunks remained in storage for years. Some were never claimed. In 1865 Smith sold his entire stock of provisions and groceries to James Fell (see next page) and then leased the property.

Madame Lacharme, owner of the Colonial Market on Johnson Street between Government and

Store streets, placed an ad in the *Colonist* on October 28, 1861, offering inducements to shop at her place:

Madame Lacharme respectfully invites the ladies of Victoria and the public generally to pay a visit to the Colonial Market and inspect her preserves of every description; vegetables, fruits and marmalades of Island production. Madame Lacharme has employed a skilful Butcher who prepares and dresses Meats in every possible manner ... and has also made arrangements with the Italian fishermen to be supplied with fresh fish twice daily ... and having a new coffee grinding apparatus ... sells the best ground coffee, French style. Chickens in coops, eggs, butter, put up for the Upper country and ready for shipment.

Henry Saunders arrived in Victoria in 1862 and almost immediately was put in charge of a grocery owned by P. Manetta on Johnson Street. He bought out Manetta and formed a partnership with Giraud Promis, who already had a grocery and provision store at 55 Johnson Street. This partnership lasted for two years, after which Saunders remained as sole

James Fell, 1886.
BC Archives A-01299.

Fell & Company store at the corner of Fort and Broad streets, about 1880. James Fell stands in the doorway with partner Henry Moss. BC Archives D-03913.

proprietor until about 1901 when the firm was converted to a limited liability company with Saunders as manager. He died in 1904, but the company was still in business in 1910 with his son as owner.

James Fell arrived in town at the same time as Saunders. Fell had been a tea, coffee and spice merchant in London and Liverpool. Following a side trip to the Stikine, he returned to Victoria and established a coffee and spice factory on Broad Street. Fell modestly claimed to rival the best grocers on the west coast. His advertisements specifically mentioned the quality of the coffee and spices, cautioning buyers to get their supplies "directly from the manufactory in Broad Street near Fort" rather than be disappointed in the "stale productions" from California that would result in "death in the tea pot" (*Vancouver Times*, November 5, 1864). Fell bought the Red House

Grocery from Charles Bayley in 1865 and expanded his business into a general grocery store.

In 1868 John Finlayson became Fell's partner. The firm of Fell and Finlayson continued selling staples, fresh meat and fresh vegetables, not only to the townspeople, but also by contract to such places as the city jail, the Fraser River light ship and the lighthouse at Race Rocks. This partnership carried on until 1872, when Finlayson left to open his own grocery on Government Street. Fell continued his business at his original Broad Street location until 1878, when he purchased the southeast corner lot at Fort and Broad streets. This had been a part of the unsuccessful public market of 1861 (see page 129). He demolished the brick building that had remained there from the market days and erected a two-storey structure described in the *Colonist* (September

Interior of Fell & Company, about 1900.
BC Archives D-03912.

On November 24, 1887, the *Colonist* copied a note from the *Albina Courier* in Oregon that may have alerted the local grocers:

Arrival of Skedaddled Grocers from Oregon. Skipped: Mssrs Fletcher and Graham the grocers, who are "English, you know" have skipped to Victoria, leaving numerous creditors to mourn their hasty departure.

Copas & Young on the southeast corner of Fort and Broad
streets, Victoria, 1912. BC Archives D-02224.

1878) as being "more substantial and extensive in
character" than its predecessor. The lower floor was
occupied by the grocery and the upper floor by the
Royal Hotel.

In partnership with his son-in-law, Henry Moss,
Fell ran his wholesale and retail grocery from this
location, until his death in 1890. He carried a fine line
of provisions for the time. As an ardent spiritualist,
Fell placed an ad in the *Colonist* on December 4, 1880,
warning: "During the perihelia of the planets people
should be cautious of what they eat and drink." In
1895 his wife, Martha, and sons, James and Thornton,
incorporated the firm in collaboration with Henry
Moss and James Morley, offering shares at $100 each
for a company whose capitalization was $75,000. Fell
& Company continued until 1908, when Copas &

Young took over the business.

Copas & Young had scarcely settled in to the
building when it suffered damage from a fire that
had possibly been set by an arsonist. But in June
1908, the firm announced that its business had
increased so much that it had doubled its staff. The
company advertised itself as an "anti-combine"
grocer, one who remained independent of grocers
who had joined together to share favourable dealings
with the suppliers. Copas & Young was one of the
first grocery stores to close on Wednesday afternoons
in the summer, freeing its staff to enjoy a picnic. The
owners hired a tally-ho and took all their employees
with "their lady friends" to Sooke or Colwood or
Goldstream where they had an evening meal followed by games and other recreation.

Interior of the Dixi H. Ross grocery store at 111
Government Street, 1911. BC Archives F-06964.

King Edward VII 10-cent Piece
This new Canadian coin will be given
in change with every purchase this
week. Be sure and get one.
– Dixi H. Ross advertisement,
Colonist, October 23, 1902.

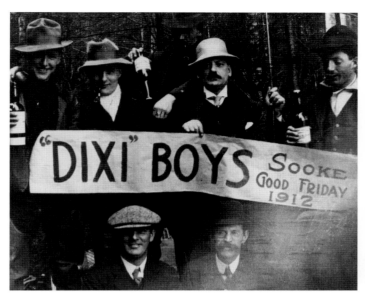

Staff of Dixi H. Ross grocery store at a grocer's picnic. BC Archives F-06965.

Carne & Munsie Family Grocer store in the Odd Fellows' Building at the southeastern corner of Douglas and Johnson streets, 1892. BC Archives D-07087.

An advertisement in the *Colonist* on June 23, 1895, announced: "Our name is over the door. Our reputation is established. Our prices are unapproachable." The name over the door on Government Street was Dixi H. Ross, and the reputation was excellent. Ross sold his groceries for cash and invited customers to have a cup of tea while they placed their orders.

Ross was an American who had lived in the Cariboo for some time and worked for his uncle who owned several stores in the region. When he came to Victoria he entered into a partnership with J. Cameron and then with F. Neufelder before opening his own grocery in 1875, located at 117 Government Street. When Ross retired in 1899, his son Harry became manager and a few years later moved the firm to 111 Government Street.

The interior of the store at this time had long oak counters, plentiful stock and a large selection of wines and liquors. (The counters were made by Weiler Furniture Company, a well-known business in the city.) A large warehouse at the rear opened to an alleyway on Johnson Street. The liquor department, for which the firm was famous, faced on Broad Street. Great pride was taken not only in the service given the customers, but also in the fine harness and matched teams of the delivery wagons. The firm closed in 1916, possibly foreseeing the dramatic decrease in revenue that would be suffered by the extensive liquor department as a result of Prohibition.

Experience in one company sometimes led to the opening of another. For seven years, H.O. Kirkham was the manager for Dixi H. Ross. In 1910 he left to start his own grocery. Kirkham bought the grocery firm of J.W. Speed, which had been established about 18 years previously. He promoted the grocery's frequent delivery schedule in his advertisements: twice daily on week days and three times on Saturday. He delivered to customers as far as Victoria West, the

Carne Grocery delivery wagon decorated for a parade in 1902. Fred Carne drives the wagon.
John Charles Cornish photograph; BC Archives E-04694.

R.H. Jameson Grocery on Fort Street next to the Scotch House. This was the building occupied earlier by Ninian Murray's bakery. BC Archives G-02982.

Spencer's groceteria.
Victoria City Archives 98007-12-2990.

Gorge and Hillside Farm. Kirkham accepted mail orders from a catalogue, and supplied provisions for "ships, camps, survey parties and the like". His ads (*Colonist*, March 22 and 29, 1914) also encouraged phone orders: "You are just as safe shopping at Kirkham's by phone as in person." Kirkham sold the store to Batchelors' Grocery in 1928.

Shortly after Fred Carne and William Munsie entered the grocery business as partners in 1884, an editorial in *The Industrial News* (January 2, 1886) called them "two enterprising young men … well deserving of the patronage of the public". Carne, the senior partner in the firm, came to Victoria from England in the 1880s. Munsie, a native of Pictou, Nova Scotia, began his career in Victoria at the Albion Iron Works, where he started its stove-manufacturing department. Carne and Munsie's store opened for business in the Odd Fellows' Building on the southeast corner of Douglas and Johnson streets.

Later they moved to 90 Yates Street. Not only did the partners run a lucrative grocery business, but they also owned several sealing schooners during the height of the sealing industry. Their grocery business was carried on at various addresses until the turn of the century, when Munsie left the firm to focus on other business interests, including being managing director for the Victoria Sealing Company and the Shawnigan Lake Lumber Company. Advertisements then refer to Carne's Economic Cash Grocery, reflecting the change from credit to cash.

Robert Jameson opened his grocery in 1887 at 23 Fort Street. He advertised himself as a family grocer, and promised delivery of goods to any part of the suburbs free of charge. Born in Alloa, Scotland, in 1844, Jameson moved with his family to Florida in 1845 and later to Whitby, Ontario, before arriving in Victoria to set up his business. He quickly became known in Victoria for wearing a kilt, proudly proclaiming his ancestry. His son, William, joined him in the business as clerk and bookkeeper. In 1901, Robert Jameson became a travelling salesman for Balfour & McLaren, tea importers in Hamilton, Ontario. His sons, William and Carron, took over the store and continued it under the name Rickshaw Tea and Coffee. Advertisements claimed that one pound of Jameson's Excel blend coffee would make 48 large or 60 regular cups of strong, delicious, aromatic coffee. On Spetember 25, 1908, the *Colonist* described the company's inducements to its booth at the Agricultural Exhibition at Willows Park:

> W.A. Jameson … has had a free demonstration of coffee which was served by two white-garbed lady attendants. Their tent was taste-fully decorated and the numerous shelves lined with many brands of coffee and samples of baking powder, spice and the like. The booth was crowded with people and encomiums on the coffee were freely passed to the crowd.

Shopping habits began to change after the First World War and the older establishments disappeared or merged as grocery shopping adjusted to changing consumer demands. David Spencer's department store now boasted a large grocery section with a wide assortment of goods. An early type of delicatessen opened that gave food demonstrations in the store and offered a mail-order service.

In the late 1920s a new approach to shopping appeared with the self-serve stores, such as the Piggly Wiggly and subsequently Safeway, first opening in James Bay and then spreading to other locations around the city.

This appeared in the *Islander*, a supplement to the Victoria *Colonist*, on April 27, 1980, under the title "The Colonist's Poet of Yesteryear". It did not give a date for the original, but it's clear that it was written before the advent of the self-serve grocery store.

Rowbotham
"The Grocer" is the man to see
For groceries in great variety
He the largest stock does show
And sells his goods so very low
T'will pay you well on him to call
Special bargains he has for all
For tea and coffee he is renowned
None better in Victoria can be found
A speciality of this trade he makes
And special pains with orders takes
For Butter, Eggs, bacon or Cheese
He can the most fastidious please
Hotel keepers here will always find
Goods just suited to their mind
So when you Groceries require
For Rowbotham's store enquire
All orders delivered free
Visit Rowbotham's for economy

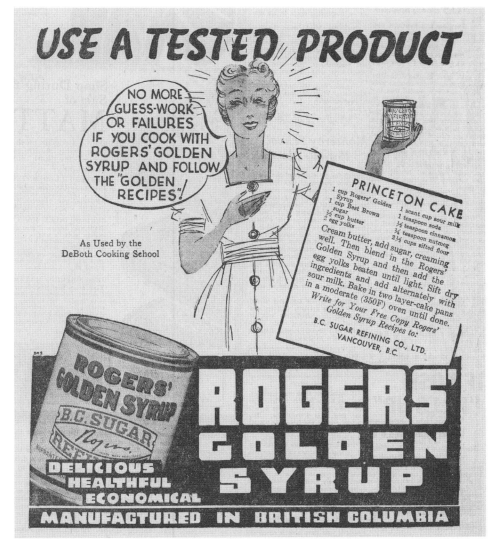

Ads in the *Colonist* on May 10, 1929
(left) and September 21, 1939 (above).

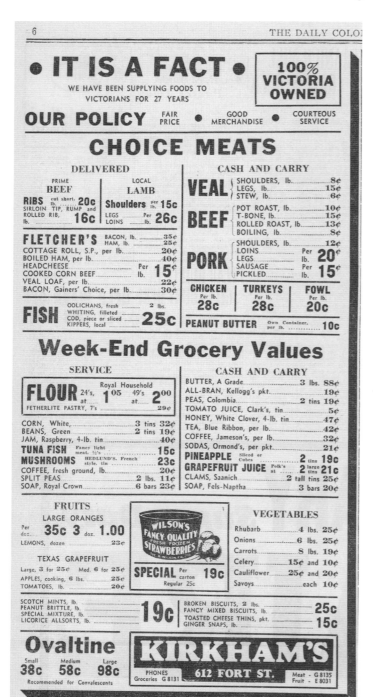

Ads in the *Colonist* on March 5, 1937 (left), September 19, 1939 (top) and August 4, 1926.

The Butchers

You heard no footsteps in the shop, only the
sharpening of knives, sawing of bones, and
bump, bump, bump of the scale.
 – Emily Carr, *The Book of Small*.

The grocers quietly supplied most of the townspeople's daily needs, but it was the butchers who
added drama by blocking streets and creating havoc
as the animals moved to the auction houses or the
slaughterhouses. Frequent misadventures arose as
the animals were driven from their point of arrival in
Victoria or Cadboro Bay. The *Colonist* reported one
such incident on September 30, 1875:

> A wild steer, while being driven up Yates Street
> yesterday, broke away from the drivers and
> made at a lady and two children standing on
> the sidewalk, who only escaped injury by climb-
> ing a low fence and taking refuge in a house. It
> would seem from the frequency of these alarm-
> ing incidents that the time has arrived when
> the City Council should step in and specify the
> hours of each day during which cattle may be
> driven through the streets of the city.

In her memoir *The Book of Small*, Emily Carr
describes a similar scene as the animals arrived at the
wharf in front of her father's store on Wharf Street
and driven through the town. The cattle, "crazed
with fright,... bellowed and plunged all over the
sidewalk, hoofing up the yellow dust." It was small
wonder that the townspeople feared for their lives
during these drives. Other incidents continued to
be reported in the newspaper. A sheep, felled by
exhaustion as the flock was moved from one of the
steamers, was placed in a lot at the corner of Langley
and Bastion where it died. Six days later, the carcass
still remained. In another instance, a pig bit a pedes-
trian as it was being driven along the street to meet
its fate at the slaughterhouse.

Victoria's early butcher shops bore little resem-
blance to modern meat markets – they looked and
smelled more like an abattoir. Imagine the ambience
created by carcasses of cattle, sheep and pigs hanging
from hooks inside and at the entrance, as butchers
wearing leather aprons cut, sawed and weighed
joints for their customers. They stood on floors
strewn with sawdust to catch the blood dripping
from freshly-cut quarters. Flies buzzed about and
congregated on the meat, and dust swirled in from
the street and mixed with the aromas of fresh and
aging meat.

By 1895, though, the city had enacted bylaws
to reduce the problems with the trade. Among other
things, these ordinances prohibited butchers from
cleaning hides on the street and letting offal flow into
the sewers. The city also began shop inspections to
curb the sale of spoiled meat. Later, the introduction
of refrigeration helped bring about the "sanitation"
of the trade.

Kenneth McKenzie's farm at Lakehill, near Victoria, about 1885. BC Archives G-07614.

At Christmas, butchers provided the town with an evening spectacle. The week before, they lit their shops brightly with gas lights and decorated their hanging carcasses in elaborate ways. Families could wander along Government Street and enjoy the scenes, perhaps stopping to order a joint for Christmas day. The newspapers waxed poetic in their descriptions of these displays. On December 24, 1876, the *Colonist* reported:

> Great must have been the "slaughter of the innocents" at Fred Reynolds' shambles. Gigantic porkers, mammoth beeves, fat sheep, frisky lambs, frolicsome calves and plump suckling pigs adorn his stalls ... saddles of mutton

which are exquisitely adorned and lettered, and a boar's head with "Happy New Year" across its capacious snout.

Continuing along the street to another butcher shop families might have found, according to the *Colonist* (January 6, 1874), that "even Bruin, the black muzzled guardian of the lonely glens beyond Sooke or Comox has been slaughtered to lend his presence to the great show.... They were all BEAUTIFULLY ILLUMINATED with wax candles on every carcass."

Victorians differed in their opinions of the Christmas displays in butcher stores. Helen Hood, born in 1878 and interviewed in the early 1960s by Janet Cauthers (for *Sound Heritage*), commented that

An almost intolerable nuisance exists ... caused by the want of drainage in the shape of butchers' offal and decayed vegetables. In the absence of sewage, we hope our friends the butcher and the vegetable dealer will not increase the unpleasant exhalation ... by mixing up more refuse with the mud and water already there.
– *Victoria Press*, April 20, 1861

And a few month's later:

The fish stalls ... early in the morning the stench arising is fairly overpowering.... The offal of the fish and other filth ... is dumped by the fishermen into the vacant water lot at the end of Wharf Street. Will not the Police Department look into the matter?
– *Colonist*, June 15, 1861.

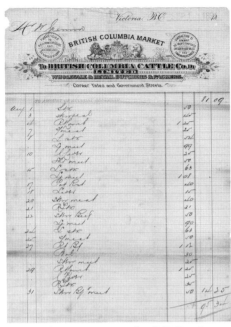

BC Market invoice to the BC Cattle Company, 1891. RBCM 2000.33.42.

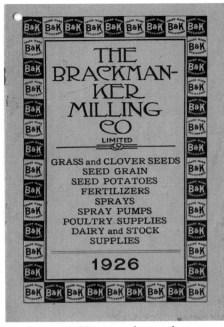

Brackman & Ker supply catalogue (see pages 99–105). RBCM 965.2216.1.

the butchers "took such pride in their meat. You'd really think this thing hanging up, this pig, was the most beautiful thing at Christmas. It had little bits of holly hung around, you know, and a little coloured flag, that sort of thing." But in *The Book of Small*, Emily Carr remembers the display in Goodacre's shop quite differently:

> Naked sheep had bunches of coloured paper where their heads ought to have been and flowers and squiggles carved in the fat on their backs.... Baby pigs looked worst of all – pink and naked as bathing babies, their cheeks drawn back to make them smile at the red apples which had been forced into their toothless sucking mouths.... Father saying, "Fine display, Goodacre, very fine indeed!"

Butchers offered the most exotic of meats during the Christmas season. One butcher offered two angora goats. The Christmas Bear, as it was called, appeared in some of the markets. For Christmas 1879 the *Colonist* reported that the "celebrated bear, the Czar of Russia", which had been captured and raised by engineers building the Canadian Pacific Railway until it reached the weight of 500 pounds (about 230 kg), was on exhibition and for sale at John Goodacre's shop (January 14, 1880). The newspaper had described it on December 22, 1879, as "without a doubt the largest and fattest French bear from the Royal City ever exhibited in Victoria and the only visible thing that has passed through the tunnels of the CP Railway" – the reporter's last comment reflected the public's impatience with the slow progress in building the railway).

Bear meat was not cheap. It sold at 50 cents a pound in 1876, while beef was 12½ cents a pound and venison 5 cents a pound. Not only was the meat for sale, but also bear grease. Bear grease was an important component of Pomatum, a perfumed aid to beauty. Quantities were exported to London where, the *Colonist* claimed, Her Imperial Highness, the Duchess of Edinburgh, "made exclusive use of it in her boudoir" (January 14, 1880). Not all bears were delivered to the butchers as carcasses. Susan Crease spoke in her personal reflections of walking home from church in the Fernwood district and seeing a bear that had escaped from the butcher's yard where it had been chained up for a few days.

Steamers bearing live animals landed at Cattle Point and at the steamer docks in the harbour. In the early days the shipments came from the Territory of Washington and the San Juan Islands. The transportation of cattle, sheep, and pigs on the steamers required great care if the animals were to arrive in good condition for auction. Several men were put in charge of the welfare of the stock. A charge was levied against them for each animal that was dead on arrival. Chickens endured their last days in coops on deck. Large animals were sometimes also shipped on deck, but more frequently they were in the hold under very difficult conditions. In spite of this the cattle from one shipment were described as "full of life and frisky", which would explain the problems with moving them through the streets. This same shipment proved to be hard on the hogs – the *Victoria Daily Chronicle* reported on February 10, 1864, that they "appeared very much fatigued" when they were unloaded.

Poaching and smuggling also existed alongside the legitimate market. In Cadboro Bay, a legal entry point for animals, two canoes laden with sheep from the American side landed one night in 1888. Customs officials arrested the smugglers as they attempted

> He [a man named Simmons] will be charged 80 cents a head for every sheep that dies on this passage ... on fulfilment of the above contract he is to receive from Dr Tolmie seven hundred & fifty dollars.... Two careful men ... are to be put aboard by Dr Tolmie to assist in taking care of the sheep during the voyage.
> – Fort Victoria Correspondence Book 1844–45.

to dispose of the sheep. An attempt to sell a brace of geese illegally hunted in 1895 resulted in a $25 fine for the vendor.

A cattle-stealing case that particularly interested the city in 1882 involved John Dooley, partner in the well-respected firm of Goodacre & Dooley, and William McNeil, a one-time employee at the Pemberton farm. Dooley was charged with receiving six stolen cattle from the Pemberton farm and slaughtering them. Pemberton placed notices in the paper offering a reward for information about this crime and he went from one butcher shop to another talking with the butchers and describing the cattle. It was on his conversation with Dooley that the final verdict would stand.

As the story unfolded in court, it appeared that McNeil spent considerable time at Goodacre and Dooley's butcher shop and was known for being in debt. Dooley was reported to have been to Pemberton's property several times and to be familiar with his cattle, but this was not an unusual practice for butchers. Edward Shields testified that he had gone out that night with McNeil to help him drive cattle and that they had opened the gate at Pemberton's and taken the cattle to Dooley's corral at Spring Ridge and left them there. The next morning McNeil told Dooley that there were six cattle at the slaughterhouse. Dooley bought them for $75 and then, with McNeil's help, killed them.

The jury had to decide if Dooley knew about the theft before Pemberton spoke to him concerning it, in which case he would be guilty of receiving stolen property. In just ten minutes (as reported by the *Colonist* on June 17, 1882) the jury found him innocent of knowingly buying stolen cattle and the case was dismissed.

Laumeister and Armstrong's Victoria meat market, about 1875. BC Archives G-02521.

Local butchers contracted suppliers on ranches around Victoria and on the mainland, but until refrigeration was available, the meat had to arrive on the hoof. Small numbers of animals were raised locally in James Bay and in Saanich or Cedar Hill. The butchers sometimes named the source of their meat when they advertised, signifying it was fresh mutton and lamb from Mrs Carter, Hillside Farm, or perhaps suckling pigs from M. Phillips or Mrs Snow in James Bay.

Cattle raised on ranches on the mainland had to be driven over bad roads to reach a sea port. On September 30, 1875, the *Colonist* reported that one driver refused to bring more cattle from the interior until the roads were improved:

> Fifty-four head of cattle from Similkameen were brought down by Mr James Allison last evening. They are consigned to F. Reynolds and Stafford & Goodacre and are fine beasts. Ninety four head, in all, were brought down to New Westminster. Mr Allison drove the band over the road from Hope to New Westminster,

Price of Chicken
1858 $1.25 each
1879 .50 each
1914 .35 per pound

Price of Bacon per Pound
1858 30–35¢
1878 20¢
1894 14–25¢
1908 25¢

Price of Sausages per Pound
1870 17¢
1914 25¢

Price of Venison per Pound
1858 10–15¢
1878 $1.00 hind quarter
25¢ fore quarter
1895 6–10¢

and found it in an almost impossible condition, and no repairs underway. He says he shall not attempt to bring any more cattle over that road.

Small butcher shops killed the animals behind the store, while the larger concerns, such as Harris or Goodacre, owned slaughterhouses in or around Victoria. Most of the slaughterhouses in town were along the wharf, and there was one at Cadboro Bay, where cattle could be landed conveniently at nearby Cattle Point. Nobody wanted an abattoir near their neighbourhood. The *Colonist* argued that the slaughterhouse near Central School was very unhealthy for the children. Smells from the slaughterhouses mingled with the pungent odour from Pendray's soap factory, and the odours rising from the James Bay tidal mud flats, created an appalling stench.

Not all meat entered the town alive. Barrels of salted pork and beef and cases of Yorkshire ham came from England, California or Hawaii. Advertisements made a clear distinction between preserved imports and fresh meat.

Poultry could be found in butcher shops, but some merchants dealt exclusively in birds, although they might also sell fruit. Some of the birds were raised locally, but many were imported, arriving in coops on the decks of the steamers from California, Oregon and the Territory of Washington. The *Colonist* once reported that chicken coops were thrown overboard in the vain attempt to save a drowning sailor;

the report did not mention the fate of the chickens.

At first, butchers in Victoria sold chickens and turkeys only as whole birds. A chicken cost about $1 in the 1860s, while a turkey might cost $4 to $6. Small wonder that Edgar Fawcett wrote in *Some Reminiscences of Old Victoria* (1912) that families could not afford a turkey for Christmas "but instead geese, wild or tame, took their place". Tactics designed to make the bird appear plumper included slipping a straw under the skin and blowing air into the space. This led one reader to ask the editor of the *Colonist* (December 22, 1881), "What can be more loathsome than the thought of eating a turkey puffed up with the foul breath of an unhealthy person?" In the 1880s, butchers began selling poultry by weight.

Butchers acquired game in season from aboriginal, sport and professional hunters. Wild fowl and game were widely advertised and continued to be available in the local markets into the 1930s. Venison was sold in the butcher shops as small cuts and in quarters. In 1859 James Bell wrote to his half-brother in Scotland (O'Reilly family papers):

The market is supplied with plenty of venison. Deer are quite plentiful. Until the arrival of the American hunters, the old residents seemed unaware of this fact. There are an abundance of water fowl, ducks, geese and even swans, but with the exception of grouse there is little feathered game inland. Occasionally a hunter brings in a black bear, but they are not plentiful.

Demetrius K. Chungranes's shop at 608 Broughton Street, about 1900, where he sold fish, poultry and fruit. A case at the front of the shop displayed poultry, pheasants and other birds. BC Archives D-05585.

An advertisement placed in the Victoria Daily Chronicle on September 3, 1863, by Birney's Game and Vegetable Store on Government Street near Humboldt piqued the curiosity of the town. They claimed to have 2000 pounds (900 kg) of very fine elk meat for sale. The remains of a "monster elk" that had been brought to town by two hunters from San Juan Harbour were displayed in the store. The ad stated:

> The animal when alive must have stood 10 feet high to the tips of his antlers and weighed 1100 pounds. The hind quarters are as large as those of a large-sized ox; the head and antlers weigh 87 pounds; the heart 9 pounds. The antlers are 12-tined and 4½ feet in length.

Game was particularly plentiful at times. On October 29, 1863, the *Victoria Daily Chronicle* reported: "Every store was crammed [and every aboriginal person was] bending double beneath the weight of game…. Surely we are revelling in the fat of the land, for game that in more settled countries is considered a luxury even by the rich, here goes a-begging for customers."

Stages ran to Saanich, taking hunters to within a mile of Elk Lake where it was reported that black bears, white cranes, geese, ducks and two kinds of grouse abounded. A party of Frenchmen who were engaged in commercial hunting in the area were killing two or three deer a day, and occasionally obtaining a black bear to be sold in the city markets. Even a cougar found a ready market.

Small game and birds were not always as plentiful. Packing the game down to the Victoria market over trails meant that the business was not particularly profitable. In town, venison sold for 10 to 12½ cents a pound, duck for 25 to 50 cents each and geese for 75 cents to a dollar each. Both household accounts and newspaper retail price lists were very specific as to what each type of wild fowl cost: widgeon, teal, mallard, pigeon, willow grouse (or ptarmigan) – each had its own price.

This notice appeared in the *Victoria Press* on December 22, 1861: "Shooting Match on Christmas Day … for 100 turkeys … distance of 100 yards …. 50 cents a shot." And this one in the *Victoria Chronicle* on January 1, 1864: "Shooting Match at Henley's Clover

Up-to-Date Fish Market, about 1904.
Victoria City Archives 98103-01-4678.

Price of Smoked Salmon per Pound	
1878	12½¢
1899	15¢
1904	20¢

Point Hotel: Turkeys and chickens will be shot today and a shooting match for $100 a side will come off about noon."

Fish was an important part of the diet. Down at the harbour there was constant tension among the Chinese, French, Italian and Portuguese, as locals jockeyed for positions on the wharf and for customers. The Italian boats and boat houses could be found at the "New Venice" wharf, beyond Dickson Campbell & Company at Wharf and Fisgard. The Chinese kept their junks at the "New Hong Kong" wharf. "At the foot of Yates Street [was] an Indian landing," recalls Gus Sivertz in an article published in the Victoria Times in 1956, "a small floating dock where Indians could bring their canoes and wait patiently until their catches of salmon were sold."

People often purchased fish directly from First Peoples in canoes or from the other fishermen at the docks or in the streets. Fishmongers sold fish from their shops or delivered them door to door. Chinese vendors carried bamboo baskets filled with fish.

Fishing in the harbour was good, yet many of the same problems existed in the 1860s as today. Acid from the new gas works, which burned highly sulphurous coal, ran into the harbour and poisoned the fish. The use of dragnets in the Gorge threatened the fish population. North at Shawnigan Lake, fishermen netted trout for the Victoria market. In just a few days they shipped 1200 trout to the city, and concern grew that the lake would be fished out.

Unlicensed hawkers appeared in Victoria when the fishing was good, and disappeared when the fishing was poor. A healthy fish-smuggling business operated from the Territory of Washington, as fishermen attempted to avoid paying duty.

Fish curing was important in the days when refrigeration was minimal. Bloaters and kippers (herring smoked whole or gutted) were a long-time favourite of the transplanted English and were prepared in various small shops around town. In 1862 the firm of Phineas Manson & Company built

The Old Fish Market, about 1905.
Josephine Carmichael painting;
BC Archives PDP00131.

Letter from a Newcomer:
The variety and excellent quality of
British Columbia fish would be hard
in any country to surpass. The same
dealer frequently sells game, and
one is puzzled which to choose – the
savoury bird or the delicate fish.
– *Colonist*, January 1, 1891.

Bought a salmon from an Indian
woman from Saanich for 10 cents.
– Alexander MacMillan, 1890s.

Nuu-chah-nulth (left) and Coast Salish
women with potatoes and clams.
Hannah Maynard photograph;
RBCM PN 06118-A.

a smoke house on Humboldt Street near Douglas. There they dried and smoked salmon and herring for sale in local shops and for export. On September 10, 1868, the *Colonist* shared this opinion of Manson & Company with its readers: "Judging from the stock on hand, it will turn out as good an article of preserved fish as can be had on the coast." Other local fish curers sought new ways to cure fish for shipment to Hawaii and to England. One Sooke processor announced he had discovered "a way to cure salmon whole on a new principle". As a trial (reported in the *Victoria Press* on March 2, 1861), he proposed to send a 25-pound preserved salmon via the ship *Constitution* to Hawaii and back. "If it will stand the warm weather without suffering in quality the invention will be invaluable." No further reports of his experiment appeared.

"Wanted: a young man to open oysters" read the advertisement posted by the Phoenix Saloon in the *Colonist* on November 1, 1862. Victorians could obtain oysters by the sack or quart container – and they were cheap. The Songhees people peddled small Sooke oysters for 25 cents a bucket. Regular fare in homes and restaurants, oysters also featured in the many oyster saloons in the colony, where they were "constantly on hand and done up in every style" for two bits (25 cents) or less. The Arcade Oyster Rooms at Government near Johnson sold 100 oysters, fresh and in their shell, for 25 cents. Many restaurants in town advertised "oysters in any manner": raw, boiled, fried, creamed, in soup, to name just a few.

With oysters such a popular fare, oyster beds were established on Vancouver Island by 1862. These augmented the Olympia oysters brought from the Territory of Washington. When an area was found that was rich in oysters, the newspapers would announce it. On November 1, 1864, the *Victoria Chronicle* described one bed on the island about 200 kilometres north of Victoria and declared that it contained "mammoth oysters … the largest yet found on the Pacific Coast … fat and well flavoured." One

Price of Oysters
| 1899 | 50¢ a pint |
| 1911 | 30¢ per dozen |

Price of Eulachon
| 1878 | 12½¢ per lb fresh |
| 1911 | 15¢ per lb salted |

Creamed oysters were prepared as any creamed dish would be today, but oyster soufflé was a different matter.

Oyster Souffle
½ pound white bread crumbs
1 whiting [a fish]
½ pint milk
3 doz. oysters
½ pint cream
a little pepper, salt, and mace
4 eggs

Make the bread, cream and milk into a sauce. Add pepper, salt and mace. When cold add the yolks of 4 eggs, the whiting which has been pounded, then the 4 whites of eggs beaten to a stiff snow, and lastly, the 3 dozen oysters, which have been scalded in their own liquor. Put in a plain mould and steam for one hour and a half.
    – *The Feill Cookery Book*,
      Glasgow, 1907.

A thickened sauce made from the oyster cooking liquid was poured around the soufflé. This recipe served 10 people.

T. Harris & Company's Liverpool
Market, on the corner Government
and Yates streets, about 1860.
BC Archives A-03006.

entrepreneur felt confident that the local oyster trade
promised "to be one of considerable profit ere long"
and suggested that anyone with waterfront to sell
for this purpose should approach him for help. By
1884 the first Atlantic oysters were being transplanted
in waters near Victoria, with the blessings of the
Chamber of Commerce, who saw a great future in
oyster farming.

In 1860 the Hudson's Bay Company introduced
to colonists a small fish called the eulachon (or ooli-
chan). The *Victoria Gazette* (June 4, 1860) assured its
readers that this oily little fish, native to BC waters,
would be "quite an agreeable relish at the breakfast
table". The paper's praise continued:

> Put up in oil as sardines we think they would
> be unequalled. At present they are salted and
> require to be soaked overnight and toasted
> before or over a fire in the morning. Their low
> price will bring them in reach of all.

Some people claimed that eulachon oil was
better than cod-liver oil. First Peoples, who had harvested these small fish for generations, saw a market
for them and sold them in the streets, charging 25
cents for three buckets. The Chinese bought large

quantities of eulachon to salt, dry or pickle. It seemed
as though a good export product had been discovered, but eulachon proved to interest few people in
the overseas market and only a light trade to Hawaii
was ever established. In the early 1900s local markets
still sold eulachon fresh or smoked.

A colony of people used to European diets
assured the butchers of the town that they would
have a market for meat and game. Thomas Harris
was the first to take advantage of this. Harris called
himself "an 'umble tradesman". The *Colonist*, in a
historical article (July 9, 1979), said that his contem-
poraries described him as a "butcher with a bald
head and a very red face, who looks as though he
had always been accustomed to good living." Of his
family: "No one could say they were a very refined
sort of people, but kind-hearted or more hospitable
people never lived."

Like many men who came to Victoria after trying
their luck in the Cariboo, Thomas Harris stayed to
contribute to the colony both as a merchant and as
a politician. His first business venture was a slaughterhouse on Wharf Street. In 1858, he established
Vancouver Island's first butcher shop, the Queen's

Harris's Family Market is the small wooden building beside J.H. Turner's brick building four doors north of the Occidental Hotel at the northeast corner of Fort and Government streets. BC Archives A-02714.

Right: Thomas Harris, Victoria's first mayor, about 1870. G.R. Fardon photograph; BC Archives A-01332.

Market, at the southeast corner of Government and Johnson streets. The Queen's Market and Lester & Gibbs were the first to challenge the Hudson's Bay Company before it left the retail business in June 1859. T. Harris & Company advertised "all kinds of meat supplied to Hotels, Restaurants, Private Families and Shipping at short notice" (*Victoria Gazette*, June 25, 1858). Thomas Harris sold the shop and slaughterhouse to Isaac Carson in 1864. That same year the *Victoria Chronicle* (June 7 and July 6) reported that Hutchinson & Company bought these businesses and several others. In 1869 John Stafford purchased the Queen's Market and operated the business under the same name.

Competition for Harris came in 1860 when Risely & Company, a butcher shop, opened on Store Street at the foot of Yates. Risely also operated a butcher shop in New Westminster. His Victoria store was in

a frame building bearing the unlikely name of Rose Cottage Market.

In January 1867 Harris opened the Family Market in a frame building on the east side of Government Street "between London House and Cleal's". John Murray was his partner for a short time, but the partnership dissolved in 1867 after only six months. The parting may not have been entirely amicable, because when Murray advertised that his new business could be found at the Union Market at the corner of Fort and Douglas streets and at the City Market on Store Street, he also stated that he had "no business connection with Mr Harris in any way whatsoever" (*Colonist*, December 31, 1867). Harris retained proprietorship of the Family Market after he and Murray parted ways, and solicited from his customers "a continuance of the kind favours so liberally bestowed upon him the past 11 years" (*Colonist*, January 10,

Serious Accident: Mr Risely of this town, met with a serious accident this morning whilst one of his men was felling an ox, the head of the hatchet which he was using fell off, and struck him in the foot, cutting one large artery and two small ones. After the accident occurred, he walked half a mile to Messrs Langleys [a pharmacy] where he arrived in a very weak state, having lost about a half a gallon of blood. He was immediately attended by Mr Moore, who sent for Dr Dickson, when he was carried home and his wound dressed. We are happy to learn that, although in a weak state at present, he will recover.
– *Victoria Gazette*,
January 9, 1860.

Lawrence Goodacre, 1865.
BC Archives G-07944.

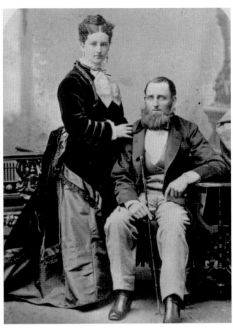

John Stafford and his wife, Maria, 1858. BC Archives G-05762.

1868). He sold the Family Market to J.H. Turner, who converted it into a carpet warehouse for the London House dry goods store, which he owned next door.

Lawrence Goodacre was born in Nottingham, England, in 1843. He left school at 16 to become an apprentice butcher, and moved to Victoria in 1866 to work as a journeyman for Stafford & Hicken. After six years in Victoria he became John Stafford's business partner when Hicken left to open his own shop on Herald Street. During this period, Stafford bought the Queen's Market, which was under the ownership of Hutchinson & Company, and moved it across the street. When Stafford died in 1882, Goodacre went into partnership with John Dooley, and married Stafford's widow. His partnership with Dooley lasted until 1888, at which time Goodacre took over the business and Dooley left for Ladner where he became a farmer. When Goodacre's sons, Roy and

Sam, joined the firm, it became known as Goodacre & Sons, continuing in business until 1923. Lawrence Goodacre died in 1925.

Goodacre's semi-serious feud with another leading butcher firm, van Volkenburgh Bros, provided *Colonist* readers with considerable amusing commentary. When the van Volkenburghs advertised that they would not decorate their Christmas meats because the decorations did not add to their quality or flavour, Goodacre replied (quoted in "Old Houses and Families" by James Nesbitt): "Should the proprietors of any City market … through lack of funds … be unable to decorate with flags, flowers, etc., we will loan our very large supply to them next week."

A report in the *Colonist* in April 1896 called Goodacre an "aristocratic" butcher not afraid to advertise his worth in glowing terms. It said that his shop was frequented by the "best clientele":

Goodacre and Dooley's Queen's Market, 1882–88,
displaying many different meats. BC Archives H-00124.

"The patrons include the leading hotels, restaurants and families in the city as well as the leading ships entering here." Service went beyond the shop itself. Goodacre himself would deliver the meat to a special dinner party, rather than consign it to a delivery cart where it would be treated to a roughness "as if fine meat were coal". At Carey Castle, the official residence of the lieutenant governor, he and the cook frequently held long discussions as to the best way to cut the meat so that it would be flavourful and juicy. Even the animals in the zoo in Beacon Hill Park received Goodacre's attention. For many years he supplied all the meat required by the zoo. Beacon Hill Park's Goodacre Lake is named for him.

John Goodacre, Lawrence's brother, was also a butcher in town. He and his partner, J.M. Lammon, established the Oriental Market at the corner of Fort and Blanshard streets in about 1868. A fire in 1870 completely destroyed the frame building, which was uninsured. Bankruptcy Court found that Goodacre's debts of $3000 were largely covered by his assets of $2700. During its proceedings, the court also looked

Stanley's Meat Market at 306 Edward Street, Victoria West.
Victoria City Archives 98801-21-4143.

into Lawrence Goodacre's finances.

John Goodacre later went into business with M. Sheppard and then with John Jackson; his partnership with Jackson dissolved in 1878. Two years later, he partnered with Edward Metcalfe at the Liverpool Market, which had been one of Thomas Harris's markets in the early days; but within a month, he sold the Liverpool Market to the van Volkenburghs. John Goodacre died in 1917.

Like Lawrence Goodacre, Harry Stanley also began his career working for other butchers. In an interview that appeared in the *Colonist* on May 13, 1930, he described his career: He began his trade in 1891 as a man-of-all-work in a butcher shop owned by McNeill and Mills, where his wage was $10 a month. When a cow was delivered to the shop one day, and no butcher was available, Stanley slaughtered the beast. The company sold the meat for a profit of $30 and rewarded Stanley for his resourcefulness by promoting him to delivering meat, and buying and slaughtering cattle at a wage of $30 a month. He then moved on to the firm of Robert

Porter & Sons where he continued hard labour for long hours. He started at 3:45 in the morning delivering meat and slaughtering animals until at least 6:00 pm. Stanley's hours only slightly improved when he entered the employ of Lawrence Goodacre in the late 1890s. At Goodacre's he worked from 5 am to 7 pm, and on Saturdays until the shop closed at 11 pm. In about 1900 he was finally able to open his own butcher shop at 306 Edward Street in Victoria West, with a stock of $30 worth of meat and one delivery boy. At that time he was the only butcher on the outskirts of the city. In 1930 the *Colonist* described him as the "oldest butcher business in Victoria still in operation".

Victoria's most colourful butcher was Frederick Reynolds. He arrived in 1861 from San Francisco, where he had been a stable boy. It was not long before he set up two butcher shops in town, the London Market at Yates and Douglas streets, and the Leadenhall Market at Government and Johnson. Both businesses proved successful. Reynolds was able to live the life he enjoyed: racing horses, wearing fine clothes, sporting a valuable gold watch valued at $325, and by his own admission pursuing some of the "flashy" ladies of the town "the same as other men, [but] not spending a great deal of money on them" (*Colonist*, June 12, 1881). He drove a fine carriage and engaged architect John Teague to build a home for him on Michigan Street.

But Reynolds had a dark secret. His real name was William Batchelor and he was a deserter from the United States Army. His good life was about to come to an end in August 1874, when his nephew,

Frederick Reynolds, 1862.
BC Archives A-06624.

Job Batchelor, arrived from England. Reynolds bought his nephew a serge coat and straw hat, and hired him to look after the company accounts. But Job kept irregular ledgers and it became clear that he was not entirely honest. At this time Reynolds's behaviour became erratic. He believed that people were hiding in his house and that he would be kidnapped and sent to China. He would at times appear naked at his front door. His fears increased, probably because his nephew knew his secret and threatened to reveal it. Job convinced his uncle to sign away all his possessions, in return for Job's promise to provide for him for the rest of his life. Job brought his brother and family to Victoria, all intent on profiting from their uncle.

Reynolds eventually regained his senses and sought the return of his property. He launched a Supreme Court case against Job Batchelor, Donald McPhaden (Job's new business partner) and Eli Harrison (Job's father-in-law). The *Colonist* (June 12, 1881) described the lawsuit, presided over by Judge Matthew Begbie, as "the most extraordinary case ever heard in the province". Reynolds sought to prove that he had been mentally unfit at the time he signed over his property and argued that all his possessions should be returned to him now that he had regained his senses.

The case fascinated Victoria for several weeks. At the conclusion, the jury found for the plaintiff and made Reynolds and McPhaden equal partners; evidently McPhaden had been unaware of the situation when he joined the firm, and was therefore innocent of wrongdoing. Reynolds's property was restored to

Spencer's meat department.
Victoria City Archives 98007-12-2991.

him and Batchelor was ordered to pay all costs of the legal action. In his summary of the case Judge Begbie expressed great dissatisfaction with the documentary evidence submitted to him, "consisting of 200 or 300 separated bits of paper of every form, substance and degree of raggedness which could perhaps be excused on the grounds of economy". His summary occupied a full page in three successive issues of the *Colonist* (November 15, 16 and 17, 1881). After the trial, Reynolds sold both his markets to Job Batchelor. Reynolds died in 1887 and is buried under the name of William Batchelor in the cemetery of St Stephen's Church, Saanich.

Some meat dealers specialized in pork and pork products. The preparation of sausages required spe-

cial equipment and careful spicing. Joseph Heywood was one such pork dealer. He opened the Yorkshire Market in 1862 at 8 Fort Street and shortly afterwards moved to Yates Street near Broad where he made pork products he called "the elixir of life". Heywood often rhapsodized about making sausages. His Warbling Pinafore sausages were produced, he said (in a *Colonist* ad, November 14, 1879), by "fifty brilliant and talented artists using two powerful water and steam engines running day and night". Jersey Lilly sausages were manufactured by "the most famous manipulators of *saucisse de cochon* now in existence" (*Colonist*, November 27, 1881). He deemed any of his sausages an antidote to sea sickness, as testified to by many ship captains.

Julius Barran, about 1888.
Hannah Maynard photograph;
BC Archives A-07195.

Brochure, 1919. RBCM 2000.33.59.

Right: Judge Peter O'Reilly's account
sheet with Lawrence Goodacre,
February 27, 1897.
BC Archives MS 2894 A01939 49/3.

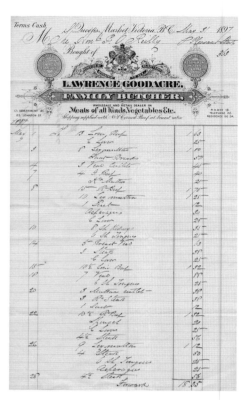

In the 1880s Julius Barran followed in Heywood's footsteps as a purveyor of pork and florid prose. He advertised himself as "Julius Barran SMA, Cantab, Inventor and Manufacturer" and "late *chef de cuisine* of the Duke of Cambridge". From his factory on Yates Street he sold the Cambridge Sausage "prepared by special permission from a recipe in the possession of the Duke of Cambridge" (*Colonist*, November 2, 1880).

Increasing concerns for public health brought significant changes in butcher shops. Refrigerated cases became available for the meat that had previously been hung out. Animals were butchered off-site and the shops no longer needed sawdust on the floors to absorb the blood that dripped from hanging meat. Nevertheless, the sawdust remained for a while as a symbol of butchers, as did leather aprons. But by the 1930s these disappeared and stores such as Spencer's had gleaming meat markets with the most modern refrigerated cases.

The Bakers

My 3 BULLY LOAVES … the largest in town … for a quarter.
— from a Bartholomew Derham ad in the *Colonist* on November 28, 1865.

The Hudson's Bay Company built Vancouver Island's first bakery in a small white-washed building outside the north entrance of Fort Victoria. In April 1849, James Douglas wrote from Fort Vancouver on the Columbia River to Fort Victoria's Chief Factor Roderick Finlayson, saying: "Happy to hear that you have manufactured Bread enough from the flour in the store to complete the victualling of the *Mary Dare* and *Cadboro*." The bakers at the fort kept busy supplying four-pound loaves of bread, several types of biscuits and flat bread for the company's use and to supply the small local community who had taken up the parcels of land offered by the company.

Victoria boomed during the gold rush of 1858 and bakers quickly took advantage of the situation. The city directory listed 10 bakers in 1860, and 20 just five years later. This budding community of 4000 to 5000 people demanded so much that local bakers could not keep up and had to import baked goods from Port Townsend and San Francisco.

Bakers had to import most of their flour, too, from Port Townsend and other towns in the Territory of Washington. Advertisements in the papers encouraged Vancouver Island farmers to sell their wheat to

local mills. But the few surrounding farms could not possibly grow enough wheat to produce the large amount of flour needed to bake the bread and fancy goods demanded by the fort, the small town, the navy in Esquimalt and the ships arriving each day in 1858 to offload their passengers and cargo.

As Victoria grew, the city's need for large quantities of bread strained the resources of the bakers. Each baker worked such long hours each day that in 1859 the Bakers' Association declared that no bread would be baked on Sunday and set out rules for journeymen who were entering their trade. The price of flour fluctuated widely as supply rose and fell, making it difficult to price the bread and still remain competitive. Many contracts fixed the price of flour at the time the contract was signed, leaving the baker open to loss if the price of flour decreased during the time of that contract.

The ships resting in the harbour or setting sail for long voyages required vast quantities of soft bread and ship's biscuit (a hard biscuit made from flour and water, meant to last for months aboard ships). Naval contracts were eagerly sought and, when awarded, advertised in the paper by the baker. The contracts guaranteed a large purchase of bread, but they were very demanding. A contract awarded to Kenneth McKenzie at Craigflower Mill in September 1861 required that up to 10,000 pounds (4500 kg) of navy bread be delivered within 24 hours of the

Hudson's Bay Company bakery, 1858.
H.P.P. Crease sketch; BC Archives
PDP01395.

receipt of the order, and that a further unlimited quantity be delivered within the next 14 days. The bread was to be delivered to the ship in Esquimalt or Victoria at the baker's expense in 100-pound bags that he had to purchase himself for two shillings each. Sometimes these bags were returned to the dock and if they were, the baker could reclaim them. Ship's biscuits were expected to remain "good and fit" for nine months or they would be thrown into the sea or sold at the nearest port, the baker taking the entire loss.

Before entering into a contract, the baker had to provide samples of his product. In 1848 the crew of the *Cowlitz* refused to accept the biscuit sent on board until the first lieutenant pronounced it to be excellent. As explained in the Fort Victoria post journal (August 16, 1848), unhappy crews could be a problem for the officers on a long voyage and so "for the sake of inducing them to continue peaceably on board, he [the officer in charge] ordered fine Biscuit or Flour to be issued to them."

An inventory of the bake house at Craigflower in 1861 listed several ovens, biscuit machines, a balance, and a baking table and trough. McKenzie employed two to eight men at this time, depending on the amount of baking needed. He also drew on navy men whose ships were idle in the harbour, paying them $1 per day with board, but this transient labour could be called back to the ship at a moment's notice. The Craigflower bake house had 58,000 pounds (26,000

kg) of biscuits in store on June 6, 1861, but this would quickly disappear if a ship needed supplies.

During the 1860s Bartholomew Derham owned a bakery at 23 Waddington Alley. Derham did not always bake what he sold. In one order, Victoria wholesale merchants Edgar and Aimé delivered to Derham's Bakery 45 cases of navy bread, 5 cases of pilot bread and 10 cases of Jenny Lind cakes, all made in San Francisco and valued at $210.82. But it was often a seller's market. Edgar and Aimé rejected one of Derham's offers to purchase bread and cakes made in San Francisco, saying, "We think we can dispose of them to other parties at a better advantage."

Derham advertised the variety of baked goods he obtained from San Francisco, sometimes showing a flair for history, as in this advertisement in the *Colonist* on December 12, 1865:

> Bread From the ruins of Pompeii: During recent excavations in the ruins of the City of Pompeii, the workmen came upon a baker's establishment in an excellent state of preservation. In the oven was a batch of bread in as perfect condition as when placed there two thousand years ago. The curious may, today, see bread the same shape and quality in the window of my establishment and I will warrant my bread will keep an equal length of time under similar circumstances. Historians tell us that bread was sold in Pompeii during the reign of Titus the Emperor for three sesterces. Now in this year

Craigflower Farm in 1860, showing the bakery (right foreground), grist mill and slaughterhouse.
BC Archives A-02936.

1865 in the reign of Her Most Gracious Majesty Queen Victoria I will sell my BULLY LOAVES 3 for a quarter, 12 tickets for a dollar.

Robert Wilson and Ninian Murray operated another bakery in Victoria in the 1860s. Wilson was a grocer and Murray the baker. They opened the Victoria Bakery at 29 Fort Street, and advertised a wide range of baked goods available to "private families, hotels and restaurants and attended to with care and dispatch". The bakery's ledger still exists and provides an intriguing glimpse into a small bakery.

The first ledger in 1865 lists the loaves of bread sold and the customers served, showing the wide range of local society who made purchases at the shop. The ledger contains the names of customers – including Sir James Douglas, bishops Edward Cridge and George Hills, and Dr John Helmcken – or simply their descriptions – such as "the stranger from San Juan", "the tall nigger woman", "the candy man" and "the man with hare lip". Most entries are for small purchases, but some customers bought large quantities – Governor Frederick Seymour bought 96 loaves one day, presumably for an official function.

Pie-ous Sailors. Five or six tars stopped one of the original piemen ... on Government Street, took possession of his can and helped themselves to the contents to the amusement and alarm of the vendor. A great crowd gathered to see the sailors munching the good things. They also forced the pieman to eat one of his own pies.... After gorging themselves ... [they] passed around a cap ... [and] collected a certain amount of money from each bon vivant and handing the pieman double the price asked for his pies, departed.
– *Victoria Daily Chronicle*, September 12, 1863.

A year later, on October 19, 1864, the *Colonist* reported that the same pieman had sold 350,000 pies in the past several years.

Looking east along Fort Street, 1860s. Ninian Murray's
bakery is the next building east of Scotch House. A
later picture of these same buildings shows the sign of
Robert Jameson, the grocer (see page 30). Frederick Dally
photograph; BC Archives A-03390.

April 1868 prices, from Ninian
Murray's ledger:

pie	50¢
Fruit cake	$1.00
Biscuits	50¢
Buns	37½¢

Jimmy the Baker. Owned to stealing
a coat from a store.... [He] was in the
early days a baker for the Hudson's
Bay Co. and was once a tolerably
decent fellow; but the demon drink
got the better of him, and first he lost
his reputation, next his situation.
– *Victoria Chronicle*,
December 5, 1862.

Central Bakery, 84 Yates Street, about 1902. The display windows feature a tiered wedding cake and a variety of baked treats. BC Archives E-01546.

Drawing by Sarah Crease of her wedding cake, dated April 27, 1853. BC Archives PDP04609.

Contracts with the navy, hotels, saloons, the police mess and the Royal Hospital provided large, steady orders while they lasted.

Murray sold bread at 12½ cents a loaf, but 10 cents a loaf to institutions holding a contract. In January 1865 his bakery sold 3,576 loaves of bread. During this profitable period he installed "the finest oven on the west coast surmounted by a chimney sufficiently high to prevent the smoke emitted from proving an annoyance in the neighbourhood" (*Colonist*, December 12, 1866). When the bakery obtained navy contracts in late 1867 its production rose to between 4000 and 5000 loaves per month. But Murray suffered through the period of economic depression that hit Victoria in the middle and late 1860s. By fall 1868 his outstanding accounts were listed at $2,250.60. One of his greatest debtors was the restaurateur and baker Daniel Cleal, who later featured in an arson trial that appeared to have its roots in his own indebtedness. Robert Wilson left the partnership at this time to establish a grocery supply business called Wilson & Company, while Murray struggled on with the bakery.

Murray's ledger recorded nothing between June 1868 and March 1869, but by this time it appears that the number of loaves sold in a month dropped to about 1000 and the business was failing rapidly. In July 1869 monthly sales fell to about 600 loaves. When the ledger was closed, the number of customers had dropped from a high of about 140 per month to 40, who bought just 253 loaves. The navy contracts and the upper society sales had disappeared. The ledger ends in February 1871 in conjunction with the last mention of Ninian Murray in the 1871 city directory. Murray joined the many business characters in Victoria who flourished for a time and then vanished.

Samuel Nesbitt and Moses Rowe Smith arrived in Victoria in the late 1850s. They each started a

Esquimalt Harbour 1868. Nesbitt built his second bakery on a wharf like these. Frederick Dally photograph; BC Archives B-00822.

Samuel Nesbitt.
BC Archives A-02367.

successful bakery business that eventually passed to the next generation.

Nesbitt had come from Ireland with hopes of striking it rich in British Columbia's gold fields. He arrived in Victoria in 1858 with enough money to open Nesbitt's Victoria Bakery on Waddington Alley near Yates Street. His pound cake inspired the editor of the *Colonist* (June 6, 1859) to "speak advisedly of the excellence of the articles of his establishment". In 1861 Dr J.S. Helmcken sold him property on the south side of Yates Street near Broad. Nesbitt moved his bakery there and installed "the latest and best machinery" (*Victoria Press*, March 3). According to Nesbitt's advertising, he sold his extensive list of products "wholesale and retail cheaper than at any other establishment in Victoria". He also advertised special baked goods for special occasions, such as matzo for Passover and hot cross buns for Easter and Christmas.

Nesbitt found it to be good business to have a second bakery near the naval base at Esquimalt. He built his Esquimalt Bakery close to the water, looking across Constance Cove to the Skinner and Craigflower farms. His choice of location proved unfortunate when, in 1867, the bakery slid into the water. He rebuilt it on rock, following what the *Colonist* (July 26, 1867) called "the old Biblical parable" of the man who built his house upon the sand rather than rock and it fell in the floods and wind. He advertised that his modern new bakery had ovens that could bake three barrels of flour at a time. When Robert Wilson formed Wilson & Company, after ending his partnership with Ninian Murray in 1868, he took over Nesbitt's Esquimalt property.

From his Victoria bakery Nesbitt sold saloon and capital biscuits for $3 a case, medium quality biscuits for $3.50 a case, soda and butter biscuits at 8 cents a pound, and sugar biscuits for 10 cents a pound. The

Moses Rowe Smith (front row, second from left) and his employees, 1892. BC Archives A-04956.

A Baker's Wages per Month

1864	$20–30
1868	$40
1875	$50–60
1892	$65–75 with board

bakery continued in its Victoria location until Samuel Nesbitt died in 1881. His wife, Jane, took over the business and expanded it. She moved it to "more commodious premises" on Fort Street between Langley and Wharf (*Colonist*, September 9, 1892), the former location of Cunningham and McBeath's bakery. Cunningham had left Victoria after what some described as a summary removal, and his business put up for auction. The auctioneer noted that while Cunningham's machinery was hand operated, it was geared for conversion to steam. As part of her expansion, Jane Nesbitt converted to steam power and brought the bakery up to modern standards.

She brought in Samuel Dickson Nesbitt as partner in 1885, and later, William Dickson joined the firm. The bakery employed seven men at this time with weekly wages totalling $120. It reported producing $30,000 worth of goods that year. The company reorganized in 1888 and became Nesbitt, Dickson & Company. The reorganization included expanding the biscuit factory at a cost of $6000, and increasing its staff to fifteen men with a monthly payroll of $1500. This expansion must have overextended the

company, because in 1890 the bakery closed, and the business, the Nesbitt home and the Esquimalt property went up for auction. Jane Nesbitt died in 1897. About the same year, after further financial reverses, Samuel Dickson Nesbitt moved to Vancouver, where he worked as a bartender, sold real estate and eventually became the manager of the Strathcona Hotel.

Moses Rowe Smith arrived in Victoria in 1858, the same year as Samuel Nesbitt. Smith came west from London, Ontario, where he had been engaged in the bakery business. Like many businessmen, he saw an opportunity to become successful in the new colony. He set up his bakery on the south side of Johnson Street near Waddington Alley. Shortly after, he moved to the north side of Yates Street between Store and Government streets.

Esquimalt beckoned Moses Smith as it had Nesbitt. The naval base promised business opportunities much beyond those in town, with 3000 men stationed there and no naval supply keeper to satisfy their needs. Two "bumboat men" named Howard and Davies asked Smith to help them supply bread and cakes to navy ships. A bumboat man was a

M.R. Smith's Victoria Steam Bakery in 1891 – "the only steam bakery in Victoria" according to the *Colonist* (January 1) – on the north side of Niagara Street between Montreal and St Lawrence streets. BC Archives B-02035.

Wagons of M.R. Smith & Company, 1890s. BC Archives C-09694.

M.R. Smith & Company employees, 1890s. Moses Smith's son, Hamilton, stands at the right. BC Archives C-09693.

small-time vendor who rowed his "bum boat" out to the ships anchored in the harbour. Essentially water-borne grocers, the bumboat men carried bread, fresh fruits, eggs, spirits and other goods for the men aboard ships to buy for personal use. They also served the prison ships. This partnership with Howard and Davies meant that Smith needed to bake 3500 loaves of bread a day. To do this, he installed four large ovens in his Victoria bakery and opened a branch in Esquimalt. Smith then obtained a contract for supplying bread to the navy, a contract he held for many years. In 1860 he bought out Howard and Davies and built a large warehouse in Esquimalt where he sold not only baked goods, but groceries and provisions.

When the naval presence in Esquimalt declined in 1863, Smith sold his interests in that part of the business and turned his attention to Victoria again. He moved to a location on Fort Street between Broad and Douglas, occupying the building that had formerly been the Royal Charter Hotel. In a *Colonist* ad on December 23, he described his establishment as a "bread and fancy cake bakery, tea and coffee saloon, etc". He also rented furnished rooms. A year later Smith moved again, but this time only a short distance to a building on Fort Street east of Broad Street.

A Kippen & Botsford ad in the *Colonist* on December 22, 1896:

The largest cake ever made in Victoria is now on exhibition in our window. It is nine storeys high, beautifully figured with cupids, and will be raffled Xmas Eve.

And in response, a New England Bakery ad, also in the *Colonist*, on December 24, 1896:

The tiniest wedding cake on record or at all events the smallest supplied in this city to fill an actual order was turned out by the New England Bakery yesterday. With icing and decorations complete it weighed just 2¼ ounces.

Price of Bread
1858	1½-pound loaf for 25¢ at the HBC bakery.
1866	1-pound loaf of milk bread for 20¢.
1879	4 loaves for 25¢ at Workingman's Bakery.
1914	a loaf for 10¢ at H.O. Kirkham.

Display of biscuits and cookies from
M.R. Smith & Company, about 1900.
BC Archives H-03569.

Settled in his final location at 57 and 59 Fort
Street, Smith expanded his clientele well beyond the
city. He shipped biscuits to the Northwest Territories
and as far away as Fiji and Australia. His dog biscuits
fed pets in Victoria and sled dogs in the Klondike.
The sealing fleet accounted for considerable business during the late 1880s. City-wide delivery kept
14 horses and small wagons busy, taking orders to
customers as far away as Esquimalt and Work Point.

Smith could not carry out all this business from
his original Fort Street bakery, so in 1891 he built a
larger biscuit factory at 91 Niagara Street with more
machinery and more ovens. This three-storey building with a basement featured the most up-to-date
machinery available, including an elevator, a feature
always mentioned when new and important brick
buildings were built in town. Smith proclaimed his
factory to be the largest north of Portland, with 35
employees. The *Colonist* (January 1, 1891) considered
the great reel oven "the most striking feature of the
whole building", at 20 by 20 feet and 35 feet tall (6 x
6 x 10 metres) "looking for all the world like a fair-
sized brick house inside the main building".

When M.R. Smith died in 1896, his sons, Garrett
and Hamilton, took over the business. They added a
confectionery plant and, in 1906, turned the firm into
a limited company. They upgraded the machinery,
explaining in a *Colonist* ad on August 12, "the old-

Popham Brothers' staff.
RBCM 2000.33.54.

fashioned cooling table is quite out of date". That year the company employed 26 women, 21 men and 5 boys with an annual payroll of $24,500. On September 25, 1909, fire destroyed the bakery, causing more than $25,000 worth of damage. The Smiths rebuilt the factory and had it running again in 1911.

Both the Agricultural Fair and the parade celebrating Queen Victoria's birthday gave the local industries an opportunity to display their products and they went to great lengths to show themselves in the best possible manner. On May 25, 1900, the *Colonist* described the Victoria Day parade float of M.R. Smith & Company:

> The design was entirely original, being built up with large soda biscuits and their popular Boston pilot bread, the top terminating with three immense sugar sticks, the whole being intertwined with red, white and blue streamers, evergreens, native flowers and Canadian flags. Inside the float were Miss L. and Master Nelson who generously supplied the crowd along the route with molasses kisses, candy and biscuits.

Described by the *Colonist* on August 12, 1906, as "a rising industry", the Popham Brothers' bakery on Mary Street in Victoria West began operation in 1906. The Pophams amalgamated their candy-making business with the Excelsior Bakery, which had been established at the turn of the century. The bakery employed 10 men, 16 women and 6 boys, with a payroll of $8400. In the same August 12 article, the *Colonist* praised it as a model bakery: "After human experience has cast the proper ingredients into the kneading trough, there is nothing left for man to do except transfer the mass ... from one machine to the other."

The Ramsay brothers came to Victoria from Toronto in 1891 to establish a steam bakery. Their advertisements, building on the pride of home industry, proclaimed these biscuits made in BC and 25 per cent cheaper than the same biscuits in the East. Soon, most of the merchants in Victoria sold Ramsay Bros Empire Cream Sodas and Princess Chocolates. (See pages 140 and 141 for examples of Ramsay and Popham biscuit tins.) Later, Ramsay Bros & Company became the Dominion Biscuit Company and bought the Regal Biscuit Company of Calgary.

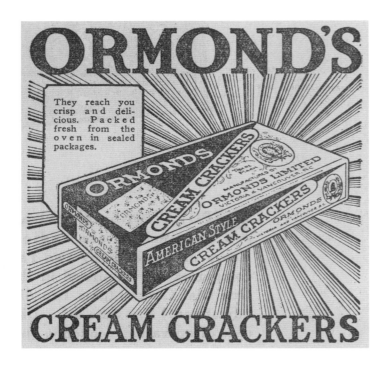

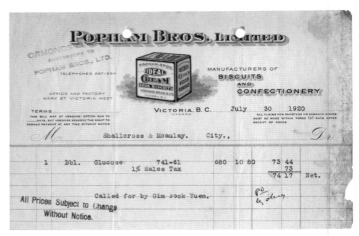

Popham Bros invoice, 1920. The Popham brothers left the biscuit trade in 1917, and the plant manager, Albert Ormond, took over the business. RBCM 2000.33.43.

Left: Ad in the *Colonist*, December 8, 1926. (See page 140 for colour packaging and advertising.)

Ad in the *Colonist*, November 17, 1931. Canadian Bakeries was one of the larger bakeries in Victoria in the 1920s and 1930s.

Water and Other Beverages

Hard to get, to drink, to wash with ... water in Victoria.
— *Victoria Gazette*, June 30, 1858.

In a land of abundant water it seems strange that water was a problem in Victoria, but the Fort Victoria Journal in 1843 recorded the struggle of Hudson's Bay Company employees to sink wells capable of supplying enough water for the fort and the ships they were expected to provision. It was difficult to find wells that provided drinking water that did not taste of clay, although in 1846 the journal reported that "the cattle will drink" from some of them (Fort Victoria Journal). The men of the fort often bailed out the wells in an effort to improve their potability. Perhaps they would have been even more discouraged had they known that the search for good quality water would last another 40 years.

The men dug wells within the fort and outside the palisade. The first four wells near the fort were not satisfactory, although one well about 400 metres north did provide better quality water. In 1850, James Douglas reported (Fort Victoria Letters): "We therefore transferred our operations (digging wells) to the Valley of a Winter rivulet ... where we hope to find ... fresh water ... for use in the Summer

> One of the oldest water routes in Victoria, bringing the owner over $200 a month, the horse, harness and cart in complete order. If applied for immediately will be sold at a bargain.
> — *Victoria Press*, May 15, 1860.

and ... make further trials more immediately in the vicinity of the Fort." The small stream there supplied water in the summer when the other wells had gone dry. It provided "excellent" water compared to the brackish water they so often found.

Later that year the HBC located a water source at Spring Ridge, three kilometres northeast of the fort, near what is now Fairfield and Vining streets, that proved to be the most reliable source for the fort and, later, for the town. The HBC considered this land to be community property and allowed everyone to pump the water. In 1858, water merchants drove their carts to the springs daily. They filled their barrels using pumps installed and guarded by one of their own men and then set out on their rounds selling water at 25 cents a bucket to the townsfolk. The Chinese built small shacks around the springs where they boiled up pots of water for laundry work, and as the *Victoria Gazette* reported on July 30, "were busily engaged in the art restorative of soiled linen".

Entrepreneurs realized that there was money to be made if they could find a water supply of some quality to pipe into the city. In a *Colonist* ad in 1858 a man claimed to thoroughly understand how to bore artesian wells. All he needed was a man with small capital and, he said, operations

Victoria's Water System
Artist and date unknown; BC Archives PDP01586.

> Water was obtained from wells and brought to the school in a barrel on a set of wheels.
>
> – James Anderson memoirs

could commence immediately. He must have been delighted when the report flew around town that a man digging a well had also found a gold nugget.

On May 7, 1861, the water merchants pulled in to the Spring Ridge as usual, only to find eight men enclosing the springs with a fence bearing the notice: "Water ... 1 bit per load." A man posing as a policeman challenged them and the water carriers retreated to the town. Two days later, the *Victoria Daily Press* reported how the authorities responded:

> The fence built around the Spring on Tuesday was pulled down yesterday morning or the night previous. Consequently the water men obtained their loads and returned to town in procession to supply their customers as usual. Upon their return for a second load, they found a bonfire made of the fencing.

The background for this soon came to public attention. George Hunter Cary, the colony's attorney-general and a representative in the legislature, had arranged to lease the springs from the Hudson's Bay Company even though the company had set aside that land for public use. The people of the town felt betrayed by Cary's attempt to monopolize the water supply. Editorials and letters to the editor quickly took the side of the water merchants. It appeared that the HBC had the legal right to sell the land around the springs, but not the six acres that had been set aside for public use. Appeals to Governor Douglas failed; he claimed that the land was no longer under his jurisdiction. But public indignation led to the failure of Cary's monopoly attempt, and free access to Spring Ridge resumed.

Cary was not the only businessman who hoped to profit from supplying the city's water. A local committee approached the House of Assembly for permission to form a water company. They estimated they would charge one cent per gallon and were bold enough to ask for a 50-year monopoly. The House replied that they needed more accurate data before they could give an opinion on this proposition. A letter to the editor railed at the idea of a monopoly and declared the cost too high. The proposal appears to have been shelved.

A Spring Ridge Water Company delivery cart filling up
with water at a pump on Government Street, 1870s.
BC Archives A-02653.

The water available in the city was not known
for its purity and "animaliculae" appeared quickly in
standing water. On July 14, 1861, a letter printed in
the *Victoria Daily Press* suggested a solution:

> The remedy is simply to reduce the temperature
> by means of ice to below fifty degrees, and all
> insect life is at once destroyed and settles to the
> bottom in the shape of sediment. Thus a small
> piece of ice put in a barrel of water every morn-
> ing not only prevents insect life from generat-
> ing, but preserves and renovates the flavour.

The first successful alternative to Spring Ridge
started operations in 1862 at Belmont Lagoon in
Esquimalt. The Spring Vale Water Company supplied ships in the harbour at the rate of $1.25 for 200
Imperial gallons (909 litres). The company built a
special sailing vessel with a 10,000-gallon (45,000-
litre) tank to carry water from Esquimalt to Victoria
where it was pumped into another large tank on
Union Wharf; from there the water could be distributed by water carriers.

The first water to be pumped in Victoria came
from a pond in the city in 1860 and was carried
through pipes made of logs that had been bored out
to a diameter of 15 centimetres. This was probably
from a spring source near Wharf Street.

In 1863, Coe & Martin Company became first
owners of Spring Ridge water. They laid water
mains along Government Street between Fort and
Douglas and also on Johnson and Yates streets down
to Wharf. The water mains were supplied by a pump
installed at the Springs. The company placed a notice
in the *Colonist* on March 10, 1864, asking anyone
who wanted water to subscribe while the streets

Constructing Victoria's water system at Beaver Lake, 1886.
BC Archives B-08079.

Below: Sections of a log pipe used in Victoria's water system in the 1860s.
RBCM 1971.245.1, 2.

were open and the pipes could be easily reached. It based the charge for piped-in water on the area of the house. Coe & Martin also announced that it would deliver water on carts to any house in the city at the rate of 50 cents a week for two buckets of water delivered each day. The Spring Ridge Water Company, under various owners, managed the city water system throughout the 1860s and into the early 1870s. When the springs ran dry in the summer, the town resorted to drawing water from Harris's Pond on lower Pandora Street, but by August or September this source was often low and the pond became a muddy pool.

Off and on through the years, letters to the editor of the *Colonist* pointed out the need for a better water supply, not only for quantity, but also for quality. In 1872, Thomas Bulkley, chief engineer of the provincial government, published a comprehensive report on the state of the city water and the need for improvement. In it, he dismissed the Spring Ridge Water Company by saying, "This Company does

not appear to have received the entire support and confidence of the public." He went on to provide statistics, a chemical analysis of the water and testimonials as to the value of soft water. Experts, he said, guaranteed that soft water reduced the chances of urinary and dyspeptic diseases, and it cooked meats and vegetables in less time. In addition, tea was more cost effective, the price per week decreasing from a 12 to 7 pence.

In 1875, the city acquired the rights to Beaver and Elk lakes, two connected lakes north of town. It dammed Beaver Lake and laid 12-inch (30-cm) cast-iron pipes through more parts of the city. The water was filtered before entering the system, but the quality remained poor for the next 40 years. Water carriers continued to deliver Spring Ridge water from hydrants to homes not attached to the pipes.

Emily Carr described Victoria's water problem in *The Book of Small*:

> Those Victorians who did not have a well on their own place bought water by the bucket

In 1877, Government House requested a pipeline to the house and gardens in return for $225 a year for five years. The city turned down the request in this way:

> The Mayor and Council regret that the funds at their disposal will not admit of the extension of water mains to the Government House this year…. [This] can only be done on the same basis as to any private consumer, the amount which you propose to pay not being so much as some private persons are now in the habit of paying, and who take the water without any special stipulation.

Water tanks in Victoria, 1895.
Albert Dresser photograph; BC Archives I-50523.

from the great barrel water-cart which peddled it. Water brought in wooden pipes from Spring Ridge on the northern outskirts of the town was our next modernness. Three wonderful springs watered Victoria, one on Spring Ridge, one on Fairfield, and one at Beacon Hill. People carried this sparkling deliciousness in pails from whichever spring was nearest their home.

My father was so afraid of fire that he dug many wells on his land and had also two great cisterns for soft water. Everyone had a rain barrel or two at the corners of his house. The well under our kitchen was deep and had a spring at the bottom. Two pumps stood side by side in our kitchen. One was for well water and one was a cistern pump – water from the former was hard and clear, from the cistern it was brownish and soft.

When Beaver Lake water was piped into Victoria, everyone had taps put in their kitchen and it was a great event. House walls burst into lean-to additions with vent pipes piercing their roofs.

The quality of the water continued to be a problem. Many complaints were lodged about the murkiness caused by plant and bacterial deposits. Some doctors declared that the water was not fit to drink. In 1888 the health officer expressed concern that many people were still using drinking water from wells on their property, which could lead to illness.

The supply of milk in Fort Victoria was even more limited than the supply of drinking water. The Hudson's Bay Company imported milk cows from the Territory of Washington along with the other animals needed in the new colony. It cost $10 a head to import cattle (a considerable amount in the

Benjamin Evans's residence at Stanhope Farm, about 1890.
BC Archives F-07442.

Fresh Milk: Benjamin Evans of Cadboro Bay will deliver pure milk from the cow at 25 cents per gallon. Families purchasing the above article will be able to get cream enough from it to make their own butter and save money in the business.
– *Colonist*, July 29, 1877.

1850s), but the long-term benefits were promising, as expressed by the *Victoria Gazette* in July 1858: "By the *Panama* ten milch cows which it is hoped will tend to render the lacteal fluid more abundant and cheaper than it has been heretofore in Victoria."

The HBC built two dairies: McPhail's just outside the palisade and Dupuis's on open land several kilometres away from the fort. The men assigned to Dupuis's Dairy did not enjoy working away from the fort. Following the death of a young Songhees boy who worked there, the men became so fearful of reprisals by his relatives that they refused to go out to their work and had to be threatened with jail before they shouldered their guns and set out for the evening milking.

As the town grew, more and more people owned cows and sold milk by the pail. These

Northwestern Creamery bottle plant, 1944. Duncan MacPhail photograph; BC Archives I-00980.

Prices of Milk and Butter

	Milk/gal.	Butter/lb
1859	$1.00	50¢
1877	25¢	
1899		15–20¢
1914		45¢

"widows' cows" roamed outside their pasture and into the streets, where pedestrians stumbled into them on dark nights. Dairies on the outskirts of town brought milk in by cart and sold it door to door, scooping it into the pails the customers brought out. Merchants in town also received milk for resale.

Delivery of milk was not always ensured, even for high-ranking clergy, as Bishop George Hills describes in his diary:

> January 15, 1860: I was supplied with milk the first day or two, by a milkman who drove his cart daily in the neighbourhood. One day no one came and no milk was there to be had. It was thought to be some mistake which would be rectified, again no milk. A fresh milkman was found. The cause of failure in the other, by his own account, was that as he was a Roman Catholic he could not think of supplying milk to a Bishop of the Church of England.

The number of milk vendors in Victoria grew from 30 in 1859 to more than 380 in 1930. In the early

Milk bottles: Woodlands, about 1930; Turner's dairies, about 1940; and Northwestern Creameries. RBCM 986.37.5, 986.37.3 and 971.61.586.

Soda works in Victoria	Location	Years of operation
Paul Bocian	Johnson St	1869–71
Fairall	Esquimalt Rd	1897–1908
Greenwood & Morley	Yates St	1874–81
Louis Hautier	Johnson St	1860
Christopher Morley	7 Waddington Alley	1872–73, 1882–1911
Pioneer Mineral Water Works	Humboldt St	1859–76
Alexander Phillips & Sons	8 Yates St	1879–96
Phillips Brothers	David St	1896–98
Thomas Shotbolt	Johnson St	1864–71
Thorpe & Company	David St	1891–1923

days, neither the dairies nor their customers had any cooling facilities, so sour milk was plentiful and the colonists had many recipes for its use in biscuits, cakes, puddings and breads. Sour milk was only one problem the city had in regulating the milk supply. Not all the dairies were clean, and everyone knew that diseases could spread in milk just as well as they did in water. Someone needed to keep an eye on the milk supplier. By 1895 the city had established a health officer to inspect the dairies and register all milk vendors. Gradually, milk suppliers installed cooling facilities. By 1930 two-thirds of the milk supplied was pasteurized.

With drinkable water and milk so difficult to obtain, soda water and fruit syrups became an important part of the Victorian diet. Early in the colony's history the makers of these liquid alternatives quickly established profitable businesses. The most successful was the Pioneer Mineral Water Works, operated by Alexander Phillips and his three sons, which opened in 1859 on the south side of Humboldt Street. In 1862 he opened a second business, Pioneer Soda Works, on Fort Street.

Phillips suffered a small setback on August 17, 1860 (as reported the next day in the *Colonist*), when

Popping In and Out: A bibulous young gentleman while at the fire yesterday morning [at Russell's Grocery on the corner of Fort and Blanshard streets], made his way to the rear of Phillip's storehouse and commenced to prospect among the heaps of bottles for the wherewithal to wet his clay. For a long time he searched, and finally found a bottle which appeared to contain pop. Striking an attitude and inwardly exclaiming with Mrs MacBeth, "Come, let me clutch thee", he removed the cork and applied the mouth of the bottle to his lips. Within a second of time thereafter the infatuated man made a wry face, uttered a low cry, dropped the bottle and fled precipitately from the spot. "Pizzo!" ejaculated a bystander. "No," dryly remarked Alex Phillips, who had coolly watched the young gentleman during the operation, "turpentine, and good for worms".
– *Colonist*, July 16, 1870.

Lost an Eye: A little Indian boy in the employ of Mr Phillips ... lost an eye yesterday in a singular manner. He was engaged in bottling some of the effervescent fluid, when one of the bottles burst into a thousand pieces. A flying fragment unfortunately entered the boy's eye and deprived him of his sight.
– *Victoria Chronicle*, September 20, 1863.

Christopher Morley.
BC Archives F-00238.

Thorpe Factory, about 1900.
Victoria City Archives 98412-10-6707.

a horse hauling a load of full bottles became frightened and dashed along Yates to Government Street. By the time the horse was brought to a stop most of the bottles had been broken and their contents spilled onto the dusty street.

Drug stores and soda factories offered fruit syrups and raspberry vinegars for sale, and soda-water fountains, where fruit syrup could be added, sold popular drinks for the whole family (see page 141 for an example of a Shotbolt fruit-syrup label). Thomas Shotbolt, the druggist, owned a popular fountain shop that he opened in 1860 on Johnson Street just west of Government. Later he opened the Aerated Water Works at Cook and Yates streets.

Christopher Morley and Hills Thorpe owned well-known soda companies in town. Morley had learned how to produce soda water while working for Thomas Shotbolt. In 1872, in partnership with John Greenwood, Morley bought Shotbolt's soda factory. The partnership dissolved in 1879, and Morley

established his own business in Waddington Alley. He claimed that his new shop was the most complete soda-water factory north of San Francisco, and it possessed the modern convenience of an elevator, a recent invention. Morley used 10 tons of sugar each year. He also needed a large supply of filtered water – two carts made deliveries each day. By 1891, he advertised that his shop could produce 20,000 bottles of aerated beverages a day, as well as essences and syrups. All this was produced with a staff of nine men, each paid $2.50 a day. Crystal Springs Water Supply purchased Morley's factory in 1912 and moved the operation to Richardson Street, where the business continued until 1976.

Hills Thorpe opened a plant in Victoria in 1891. Thorpe & Company supplied a line of mineral waters, ginger ale, ginger beer, essences, syrups and bitters. The local press duly noted awards won at world's fairs in Europe, India, South Africa and Australia. Thorpe eased public concern about the

Four glass bottles for sodas and two pottery bottles for ginger beer. RBCM 1964.1766.1, 1985.34.17, 1996.16.3, 2000.48.33, 1971.61.521 and 1967.37.8.

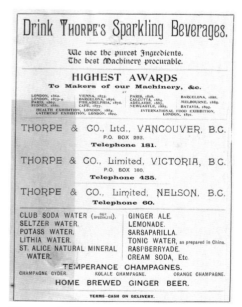

Thorpe & Company broadside. RBCM 1998.87.1.

Soda bottles of Greenwood and Morley (left), and Christopher Morley. RBCM 1964.4917.2, 1984.12.2, 1970.120.1.

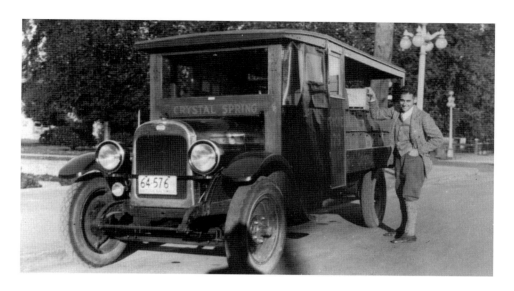

Crystal Springs delivery truck 1926.
BC Archives C-02445.

quality of the water used in production by advertising (*Colonist*, May 24, 1901) that he used only pure soda water prepared with Pasteur Berkefeld filters "endorsed by the British Medical Journal" and resulting in "limpid pure water" eliminating any possible germs. In another ad (*Colonist*, August 31, 1902), he declared that you could "ensure your health by drinking out of sweet, clean Crystal Glass bottles". Not only did the company advertise its table water as sparkling, but they touted it as a cure for gout, rheumatism, indigestion and acidity of the stomach. Thorpe pointed out in a *Colonist* ad on September 28, 1907, that the 10 men working for him produced "every kind of drink that does not intoxicate". He later modified this temperance claim when he advertised that Thorpe's pure soda was the best way to dilute strong liquors.

Other companies made soda water in Victoria's early years: In 1860, Louis Hautier placed an advertisement for his soda-water factory on the north side of Johnson Street "near the ravine". Paul Bocian had a plant on Johnson Street from 1869 to 1872. The Fairalls, father and sons, were in the business from 1897 to 1908. Coal dealers Kirk & Company

also made soda water at this time in Esquimalt. The Fairalls purchased the Kirk & Company soda water operation in 1917 and ran it until 1922. They were the first to bottle Coca-Cola in Victoria in 1919. From 1911 to 1926, Victoria & Vancouver Botanical Beverage Company produced non-alcoholic beverages at 2620 Cedar Hill Road. Business partners Alfred Ashworth and Samuel Layity delivered ginger ale, root beer and other flavours in large jugs to homes in the city. In 1909, Thomas Brooks, an ex-driver and salesman at Thorpes, began a bottling business in his home at 624 Frances Avenue.

Ciders were both imported and produced locally. In the *Colonist* on September 9, 1864, W.S. Bancroft advertised his imported apple cider in containers bearing "the autograph of W.S. Bancroft on every bottle". On September 19, 1865, a *Victoria Chronicle* advertisement drew the public's attention to Pritchard's, "the only cider mill on the Island". Pritchard pressed enough locally grown apples at his residence on Fort Street to produce several barrels of cider a day. In 1887, Savory & Company was established as a cider factory at 225 Cook Street, providing cider from local apples and competing successfully

Price of Coffee per Pound	
1858	15–19¢
1878	50¢
1900	25–40¢
1918	25–45¢

In Victoria coffee is scarce.... The price has become so enormous since last year that thousands of families have discontinued the use of coffee.
– Victoria *Daily Chronicle*, August 12, 1863.

Coffee tins. RBCM 1987.7.465 and 1987.7.469. See pages 142–43 for more examples, in colour.

with imported cider. A local import firm suggested that apples grown in Victoria would not make good cider, but turn to vinegar. Proving this wrong in its first year, Savory & Company produced 13,000 to 18,000 litres of cider, advertising it in the *Colonist* (January 1, 1887) as "the beverage which is refreshing and beneficial and will not intoxicate".

People brewed vast quantities of coffee in mining camps, homes and the many coffee saloons scattered about Victoria in the 1860s. Merchants ground and roasted the beans in their shops; others established mills that prepared coffee and spices. By 1861 advertisements appeared in the newspapers encouraging the public to buy fresh local products rather than the staler imports. In 1861 Edgar & Aimé wrote to the firm of Marden & Folger in San Francisco to explain that they were unable to profitably sell its coffee, because "the manufactory here is now selling, or rather supplying, most of the Coffee now used".

According to his ad in the *Colonist* on December 12, 1862, Innocente Ragazzoni supplied "the best

Contest poster. RBCM 2000.33.53.

Thomas Earle, 1891.
From *Victoria Illustrated*.

Earle and Stemler's new spice mill, about 1891.
Charles McMunn photograph. BC Archives G-02966.

ground coffee manufactured in this town" from his grocery shop at the corner of Yates and Douglas streets. In the following year, Ragazonni sold his grocery business and opened a shop on Johnson Street that specialized in the daily grinding and roasting of coffee. He packaged it in one-pound paper wrappings and in one-, two-, five- and ten-pound tins.

Ragazzoni declared all his products pure and unadulterated, separating himself from the many suppliers who mixed chicory in with their ground coffee (tea, too, was frequently adulterated with the leaves of other plants or even iron filings). Working on Government Street at the same time, William Burlington Smith advertised his coffee, which he ground and roasted daily, as "a first rate article, retaining its aroma and fragrance" (*Colonist*, February 4, 1862). James Fell brought expertise as a coffee and

spice merchant when he came from England in 1861; his store on Broad Street near Fort later expanded to carry a full range of groceries. Lawrence Travo appeared in the 1863 city directory as coffee roaster at 13 Johnson Street.

Like many coffee roasters, Ragazzoni also prepared and packaged spices. Coffee mills had the grinding equipment to prepare spices and often packaged their own brands. The largest spice suppliers in Victoria for many years were Jameson's of Victoria, the Vancouver grocery wholesalers Kelly Douglas and Malkin's, and the Empress Manufacturing Company, also of Vancouver. Some grocers also sold spices packed under their own brand names, including Spencer's and Woodward's.

The Pioneer Steam Coffee and Spice Company, established in 1875, was a successful business in

W.A. Jameson Coffee Company in 1912. A billboard for Ridgeway Tea is on the building to the south.
BC Archives D-04625.

Spices are all genuine and consequently much stronger than the adulterated products imported to this Colony.
– Fell & Company ad in the *Colonist,* February 8, 1864.

Victoria for many years. Its founder, Louis Stemler, had arrived from Germany via the gold fields. Initially he worked as an upholsterer at the Weiler Furniture Company, and then he started his coffee and spice business on Wharf Street at the foot of Yates. Soon Thomas Earle, who had been employed by Rueff & Company as a bookkeeper, became his partner. Earle gradually invested more and more in the business until, in 1881, he had the controlling interest. Earle was always listed as proprietor with Stemler as his partner, but Stemler was in full charge of the coffee and spice factory. Earle bought and distributed the entire factory's output through his wholesale grocery firm under such brand names as Pioneer, Crown, Star and Champion.

The word "steam" in the Pioneer Steam Coffee and Spice Company, emphasized that the firm ran a modern factory that did not depend solely on hand labour. In 1883 it enlarged and refitted the Wharf Street factory, increasing the steam power, adding a new steam coffee roaster and installing "a pair of French burr stones for thoroughly pulverizing all kinds of spices" (*Colonist,* April 26). Three coffee mills had the capacity to grind 3000 pounds of coffee a day. Stemler designed and patented sealing lids

for the jars. The factory also made the tin boxes and ornamental labels.

An advertisement in the *Colonist* on April 26, 1883, informed customers: "Our spices are picked strictly pure and put up in cans with Stemler's Patent Tops and Ornamental Labels." Later the company also packed spices in glass bottles.

The company expanded its facilities again in 1886. Earle moved his grocery to another building, and the coffee and spice operation moved to 148 Government Street.

The business continued to grow, having done $30,000 worth of business so far. In 1891, Thomas Earle bought a lot at the corner of Pembroke and Douglas streets, where he built a new spice mill. The two-storey wooden building reportedly cost $7000. It contained a plant for manufacturing tin cans and fir boxes at the back. The Albion Iron Works, a local firm, built a 20-horsepower boiler to drive the steam machinery. Now the company's range of goods manufactured included cocoa, cream of tartar, mustard, baking powder and jelly powder.

As Earle became more and more involved with the politics of the town, he neglected his wholesale grocery and the factory. In 1903 his creditors held a

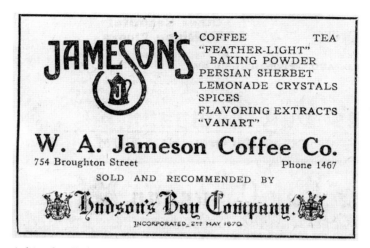

Ad in the Colonist, May 1, 1927. Jameson was Victoria's most prominent supplier at this time.

Kelly Douglas warehouse in Victoria, 1947. This Vancouver-based company was BC's largest wholesale grocery distributor. Duncan MacPhail photograph; BC Archives I-01814.

meeting, and by 1906 A.J. Morley had taken over the mills.

In a town with a large British population it is not surprising that tea was an important part of the grocer's stock. The people of Victoria could purchase tea in packets of various weights from grocers and Chinese importers. An advertisement in the *Colonist* in 1860 by Kwong Lee & Company told local merchants that 50 half-pound packages of best-quality black tea could be seen at the salesroom of P.M. Backus, the auctioneer. On April 15, 1864, Tong Fat put an ad in the *Colonist* urging families "who study economy" to purchase their tea from his tea store on Government Street.

The price of tea varied widely depending on its source (China or India) and its quality. In 1863 Young Hyson tea was 4 cents per pound while Souchong tea was 75 cents. On November 12, 1889, the *Colonist* reported that the Victoria trade preferred Indian tea,

the Chinese being "careless in handling and packing: English plantations [in India] have modern equipment". At this time Chinese tea was 18 to 35 cents a pound and Indian tea was 30 to 50 cents a pound.

Each year at the Agricultural Fair, at Willows Park in Oak Bay, merchants demonstrated their products, including tea. W.A. Jameson Coffee Company and others served tea at their booths. Dixi Ross represented its beverages well on the company's Victoria Day float in 1900, as reported by the *Colonist* (May 25), hauling a huge beer-bottle "cannon" and a carriage decorated as a gigantic package of tea "for which the firm is famous".

Jameson coupon list.
RBCM 1985.34.9a.

Fell & Company account.
RBCM 2000.33.51.

It was the food shops that Merry Christmassed the hardest. In Mr Saunders, the grocer's, window was a real Santa Claus grinding coffee. The wheel was bigger than he was. He had a long beard and moved his hands and his head. As the wheel went round the coffee beans went in, got ground, and came out, smell and all.

– Emily Carr,
The Book of Small

Java Coffee in its native purity fresh roasted and ground daily. Strongly recommended as the first rate article, retaining its natural aroma and fragrance. Warranted superior to any imported. Put up wholesale and retail. Wm B. Smith.
– *Colonist*, February 4, 1862.

The Beer Brewers

by Greg Evans

New Copper Boiler – a new copper boiler has just been finished by Mr. J. S. Drummond of Yates St, for Messrs Elliott & Stuart, of the Lion Brewery. It is capable of holding six hundred gallons, and is the largest manufactured in this city. The constantly increasing demand for the Pale Ale produced at the Lion Brewery has rendered the putting up of this additional copper a matter of necessity. This speaks well for home manufacture.

– Lion Brewery ad, March 11, 1863

In 1858, William Steinberger established the Victoria Brewery at Swan Lake. In doing so, this native of Cologne, Germany, launched the commercial industry on both Vancouver Island and mainland British Columbia. But Steinberger did not stay long at Swan Lake. In 1859, apparently because of polluted water and no doubt a desire to be closer to the market, he moved his brewery to the corner of Government and Discovery streets. Ultimately, this site would be the home of one of the Pacific coast's best-known breweries.

Steinberger quickly found himself in the company of others. In 1859, Arthur Bunster, a colourful Irishman from County Tipperary, established the Colonial Brewery. In the 1860s, the Half-Way House, Lion, James Bay and Bavaria breweries began production for the local market. The decade ended with the establishment of the Phoenix Brewery by Charles Gowen in 1868, a man whose earlier life story included a colourful career aboard clipper ships.

These pioneer brewers were a diverse lot. Some were experienced, practical brewers, while others either learned the profession upon arrival or turned the day-to-day operation to a professional in their employ while they devoted energy to other business ventures. Regardless, they found a ready and appreciative market.

Many of the people arriving in the new Colony of Vancouver Island came from countries in western and northern Europe, where the consumption of beer was culturally significant and often considered a staple of daily living. This market was strengthened by the presence of the Royal Navy and the crews of vessels stopping at the port of Victoria. All preferred fresh beer and, of course, the government of the day didn't object to the accompanying tax revenue.

While beer was being imported during this time from as far away as England, there was no guarantee that it would arrive fresh months after leaving the brewery. Even such styles as India Pale Ale, brewed specifically to survive long voyages at sea, could not be guaranteed to arrive in tip-top condition.

This placed our pioneer brewers in a good business position, and they were quick to point out the superior attributes of their locally produced products. An advertisement from the newly opened

Left: Arthur Bunster, owner of the Colonial Brewery, was also a farmer, politician and promoter of British Columbia. BC Archives E-09110.

Charles Gowen owner of the Phoenix Brewery, also served as a Victoria city councillor and volunteer fireman. BC Archives F-05110.

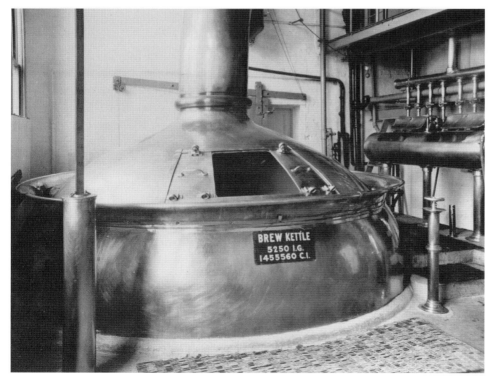

This kettle in the Victoria-Phoenix Brewery was the largest used by any of the city's breweries.
BC Arhives G-05394.

The Half-way House Brewery on Esquimalt Road,
established by James and Elizabeth Bland in 1861.
BC Archives D-01890

Colonial Brewery appeared in the *Colonist* on July 11, 1859, stating, "XX & XXX Ale, Porter and Lager Beer, always on hand, superior in quality to any manufactured on the Pacific Coast." The proprietor, Arthur Bunster, clearly intended to expand his market, because the ad went on to say: "orders solicited from all points on Fraser River, Washington Territory and Oregon and promptly attended to."

While the multitude of saloons offered local brewers a ready clientele, families at home also comprised an important market for them. An ad from the Bavaria Brewery on July 13, 1863, stated that "the Proprietor is now prepared to supply Families, Hotels and Restaurants with the Best Quality of Lager Beer." It promised that its products could be purchased "on the most reasonable terms. Orders promptly filled, and Beer delivered to any part of the city without extra charge."

Brewers delivered their beer in kegs or bottles. Some did not like to bottle their beer, because it

was cheaper and easier to distribute it in bulk kegs than to set up a more labour-intensive bottling line. Saloons preferred delivery in kegs, anyway. The breweries that sold beer by the bottle used crockery bottles at first, gradually moving to glass, which became prevalent during the 1880s.

But consumers had one other choice. They could buy it from a saloon or directly from a brewery by volume in whatever container suited their fancy – a large jug or a pail, usually able to hold two or more quarts. Many households assigned this task to a younger member of the family – the fetching of beer to accompany dinner.

James Bay Brewery owner A.J. Welch appealed directly to the market he felt offered real potential – the Royal Navy. On July 3, 1866, he invited "Jolly Tars … during the general leave – July 1st to 5th" to come to his brewery and enjoy themselves. He offered "Foot Ball, Quoits, & Dancing every evening in the large Malt House" where ale and porter could

Bavaria Brewery on Fort Street.
BC Archives E-08482.

be had for "6d per Quart!" He even arranged for buses to shuttle customers from Everett's Exchange Saloon on Store Street to his brewery. This strategy did not have a lasting effect, because the James Bay Brewery closed later that year.

Whatever their approach to marketing and sales, all local brewers faced the challenge of securing the raw materials needed for brewing. They relied heavily on imports from California and beyond, which often came at a real expense. For example, the cost of all hops imported during the last six months of 1862 amounted to $23,000 – a considerable sum at that time.

The *Colonist*, always eager to promote local agricultural endeavours, asserted that Victoria possessed the climate and the soil to grow hops, and had within its population experienced hop growers. Locally produced hops, it said, would reduce the financial burden on local brewers. Arthur Bunster and Alfred Elliott of the Lion Brewery took up the cause by offering prizes for the first crops of locally grown hops.

By the mid 1860s, hops were being grown in Victoria and on the northern end of the Saanich Peninsula (the latter continuing until 1912). Local hop producers appear to have provided the quantities and quality required by local brewers; some exported hops to eastern Canada.

Barley, however, was a different story. Despite the encouragement of Victoria's brewers, local farmers were not able to grow malting barley in sufficient quantity or with any consistency. So local brewers had to continue importing barley at considerable expense. Initially they relied heavily on barley produced in California and shipped from San Francisco. Later, most of the barley arrived via rail from the Canadian and American prairies. In 1903 brewers in Victoria imported 81 per cent of their malted barley from the USA, with the remainder coming from the Canadian Prairies and southern Ontario.

Good beer starts with good water. The local water was soft (free of mineral salts) and so highly suitable for the production of lagers, mild ales, stouts

Beer bottles (left to right): Embossed glass bottles from Victoria and Silver Springs breweries, and stamped pottery bottles from Victoria and Bavaria breweries. (Page 145 has later examples of labelled glass bottles, in colour.) RBCM 989.23.143, 967.34.9, 989.23.227 and 989.23.228.

and porters. Pale ale was a different story, because it requires hard water. Evidence suggests that local brewers used a technique called "Burtonizing", adding specific mineral combinations to the water to mimic the hard water of Burton-upon-Trent, England, the home of many famous pale ales.

No matter what style of beer, the real problem faced by Victoria brewers was the purity of water in Victoria's early years, as described at the beginning of Chapter 5. It was not so much the harmful organisms that might live in the water – brewing requires boiling the wort, which sterilizes the water – but with solids that had to be filtered out. Several brewers located their facilities adjacent to wells in an effort to ensure a constant supply of spring water. These brewers consistently assured the public that their water was pure. Peter Henning Peters, proprietor of the Empire Brewery, placed this ad in the *Colonist* in April 1885:

The Brewery is situated on Spring Ridge and is built over a well of pure, ever-running Spring water. This fact enables me to manufacture The Very Finest Brands, Equal to any Imperial ale, beer or porter.

After its initial growth in the 1860s, Victoria's beer brewing industry stabilized in the 1870s, with no new breweries opening. But the following decade brought five new facilities to town: the Tiger Brewery (in 1884, renamed the City Brewery in 1886); the Carter Brothers Vancouver Ale, Porter and Steam Beer Brewery (known simply as Carter Brothers); the Pacific Brewery; the E&N Brewery; and the aforementioned Empire Brewery.

In November 1888, Henry Smith Fairall, recently arrived from Orillia, Ontario, broke ground for his E&N Brewery at Russell Station in Victoria West. The *Colonist* reported that it would be "an extensive brewery, where English and Scotch ales will be

The Victoria Brewery, about 1885: an old-style "horizontal" brewery. This uncredited photograph appeared in the *Colonist* in 1962; courtesy Greg Evans.

manufactured. The building will be 60 x 48 [feet (18 x 14.5 metres)] and two storeys in height. Mr Fairall is a brewer of large experience, and the location he has selected could not be better, being excellent for shipping by rail and water." Over the next 20 years, the brewery would witness several partnership combinations, but eventually would be fully owned and operated by Fairall, alone or in some combination with his sons, James, William, Charles and Henry Jr.

These brewers continued the tradition of producing quality products. Professional pride was at stake and brewers strove to produce a fine product in what appears to have been an appreciative and knowledgeable market. And in 1886, the quality of beer made in Victoria was demonstrated far beyond our shores. In that year, the Carter Brothers announced that they had received "medals for the display and superior quality of their ale and porter from the Paris Exposition, the Colonial and Indian

Exposition and the British Columbia Agricultural Association; the one received from the Paris Exposition being a handsome one of solid gold."

The 1880s also brought great change to the beer-brewing industry, globally and locally. The science of brewing made great strides that decade, with several noteworthy breakthroughs. Louis Pasteur refined the sciences of fermentation and sterilization, the latter leading to the technique of pasteurization. Heating bottled beer to a high temperature (usually with steam) destroyed the organisms responsible for its spoilage while not damaging the other constituents of the beer. This procedure gave beer biological stability and increased its shelf life, making it easier to store and export.

In 1876, Carl von Linden demonstrated how gas could be liquefied, thus laying the groundwork for artificial refrigeration. Other improvements during this time included the use of steam power, the steady move to electricity, advancements in metallurgy and mechanization, standardization of bottles, introduction of automated bottling and the invention of the crown cap. All these improvements moved brewers away from the hands-on approach toward greater and more consistent production.

The physical appearance of local breweries also began to change. In the earlier decades, local breweries remained small or medium-sized and their sophistication varied according to their size. Most breweries were "horizontal style", one or two storeys – they made little use of gravity in the production flow, but pumped liquids from one stage of the brewing process to another.

In the mid 1880s the local industry began building larger breweries to include the new technologies, with more floors to enable the use of gravity in the brewing process. This decade saw the emergence of the brewery architect and engineer, both familiar with the new science of brewing. In Victoria, the buildings of previous decades, often rambling in nature and indicative of differing economic situations and personal brewing preferences, gradually vanished. Brewing had turned from an art into a science.

Not to be underestimated, however, was the impact of a growing population and their changing tastes towards lager beer. German immigrants introduced lagers to North America in the 1840s. Before then, all beer consumed in Canada and the USA was ale. The steady influx of German immigrants ensured lager's growing popularity and a steady market. Locally, the Victoria Brewery started brewing lager in 1859, and the Colonial and Bavaria breweries included lager in their product portfolios alongside ales as soon as they opened.

The makeup of the local brewing fraternity also played a role in product diversity. It represented many nationalities, with brewers from England, Scotland, the United States and Ireland working with those from Austria, Germany and Switzerland. Ale production was in safe hands with the likes of John

Local brewers John Vogel (left) and Henry Walther specialized in making lagers. BC Archives I-66345, I-77913.

Lawson, Isaac Stuart and John Leahy, while brewers from German-speaking countries, such as August Frank, John Vogel, Jacob Hasenfratz, Jacob Loerz and Henry Walther, ensured that lager was a standard part of the product portfolio.

Some brewers did not want to produce lager, which they believed to be more difficult, time-consuming and costly to brew than ale. The main difference between ale and lager (the main families of beer) lies in the type of yeast used. Ales are fermented with yeasts adapted to quicker fermentation at warm temperatures. These yeasts often contribute distinctive (and sometime desirable) flavours or aromas to the finished beer. Lagers are fermented with yeasts adapted to slower fermentation at considerably colder temperatures. These yeasts contribute very little flavour or aroma to the beer, so lagers generally turn out clean and crisp. Compared with the ales of the day, lagers tended to be more effervescent, lighter in colour, milder in taste and lower

Charles Gowen's new Phoenix Brewery, designed by August Meritzen of Chicago and built in 1892. From *The Western Brewer*.

in alcohol content. It's no wonder why lagers gained popularity, especially among families.

Brewers had to be precise when brewing a lager. The introduction of artificial refrigeration gave them (and ale brewers) the ability to adjust and control the temperature when fermenting and conditioning a lager – the latter essential, because lagers require long maturation times. Artificial refrigeration also allowed brewers to brew not just in the cooler months but all year round, and to do away with often damp cellars where they stored their products. The extra ice produced in the process found a steady market with saloon keepers and the general public.

Despite lager's growing popularity throughout the 19th century, ales maintained a healthier market share on Vancouver Island (12%) than on mainland BC (just 4%). The higher popularity of ale on the island may have reflected the ongoing presence of the British military coupled with the demographics of the population (a relatively high percentage of people from Britain), or it may have been because some island ale brewers produced light, sparkling ales to mirror the qualities of lager.

Other winds of change blew into Victoria. The single proprietorships and small partnerships that had guided the local industry through the early

Victoria Brewing and Ice Company, 1892. BC Archives D-05450.

decades were now giving way to the limited joint-stock company. By offering stock options, local brewers gained access to the capital they needed to build a new, modern brewery that would meet the growing demands of the consumer at home and compete with the large continental breweries, especially those in the United Sates.

In 1892, Ludwig (Louis) Erb and Joseph Loewen demolished much of the Victoria Brewery, which they had purchased in 1870, and built a state-of-the-art, architecturally imposing facility in its place. Designed by Seattle brewery architect Herman Steinman, the new Victoria Brewery stood six storeys tall and cost roughly $120,000 to build and equip. Just as impressive was the speed of the construction. Loewen and Erb laid the cornerstone in early March and had the brewery in full production by early September of the same year. They and their fellow shareholders had barely missed a beat.

One of Victoria's best-known brewing partnerships: Ludwig Erb (left) and Joseph Loewen, co-owners of Victoria Brewing and Ice. BC Archives G-04404, A-01275.

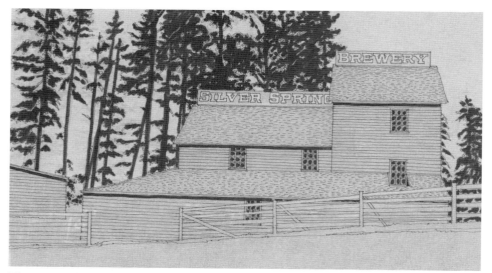

The original Silver Spring Brewery.
Rennie Knowlton illustration.

Esquimalt Brewing crockery bottle,
1915, an old-style container produced
as a promotional item.
Greg Evans photograph.

In the following year, Victoria Brewing and Ice Company merged with Charles Gowen's Phoenix Brewing to become the Victoria-Phoenix Brewing Company. Before the merger, Gowen had also reorganized Phoenix as a joint-stock company, closing down his original location at the corner of Blanshard and Yates and building a larger, more modern facility on Head Street in Esquimalt. After the merger, the Phoenix facility gradually shifted to the role of warehouse, with the production of all the brand-name products taking place downtown. But the company probably maintained a Canada Excise Brewers License for the site by brewing there once a year – no brewer wanted to give up a license.

Three new breweries arrived on the local scene in the early years of the 20th century. The Lion Brewery opened in 1901 on View Street, but lasted only two years. Much more successful and better known, the Silver Spring Brewery began production in Victoria West in 1902. The owner, Robert Tate, was a professional brewer from Ontario. Tate's ales were an overnight success, perhaps due to his expertise or to the brewery's proximity to spring water. The business expanded later in the same year through the formation of a joint-stock company that included diverse investors such as Sir R.J. and Lady Musgrave of Ireland.

In November 1908, a group of local investors reincorporated Silver Spring. This group included Harry Maynard, a former employee of Victoria-Phoenix. Maynard would eventually become one of the province's best-known brewers. With increased capital, he and his partners immediately expanded the operation by acquiring the Fairall Brothers' Brewery at the corner of Esquimalt Road and Catherine Street. Maynard set about to expand the newly purchased property and acquired the services of Richard H. Ullrich of Seattle to oversee the project. The company added three storeys to the brew house to enable full gravity-flow brewing, acquired new

Harry and Minnie Maynard, about 1889. Hannah Maynard photograph (attributed); courtesy of Joan Sloan.

Colonial Brewery label from the mid 1890s. Greg Evans photograph; courtesy of Walter Spershott.

brewing vessels and updated the artificial refrigeration machinery. The new facility became fully functional early in 1910.

The Esquimalt Brewery opened on Viewfield Road in 1914, and it was to be Victoria's last new brewery until the 1980s. Established by W.J. Hagan and James Fairall, it was primarily an ale producer. Later that year, the Esquimalt Brewery reorganized into a joint-stock company to attract new capital, but it was to have a short life. The brewery burned down in January 1916 and was never rebuilt. Arson was suspected but never proven.

Advertising kept pace with increasing demand and the competition between local and offshore brewing companies. While local brewers had always promoted their products, their earlier efforts had consisted largely of newspaper ads and signs in saloons. More and more, they used "tip" trays, sample glasses, calendars, openers, ashtrays and posters to promote their beer brands. Starting in

the 1890s, a new advertising method took hold and slowly became prevalent – the beer-bottle label. Two things aided its ascendancy: first, the steady move to standardized pint and quart bottles; second, improvements in local printing methods. In 1882, the quality of label designs increased when the Colonist Printing Company in Victoria began producing "chromatic" (colour) product labels. Using hand-engraved metal printing plates, designs became both colourful and intricate.

This rise in printing quality meant that local breweries could develop a range of distinctive product names that could be colourfully illustrated and would, hopefully, set them apart from their competitors. Shortly after the turn of the 20th century, local breweries produced and promoted such products as Ye Olde XXXX Ale, Maple Leaf Lager, Phoenix Pilsner, Silver Spray, Invalid Stout, Perfection and Jack O' Hearts Pale Export Ale, all with colourful labels. Victoria-Phoenix's Jack O' Hearts Pale Export

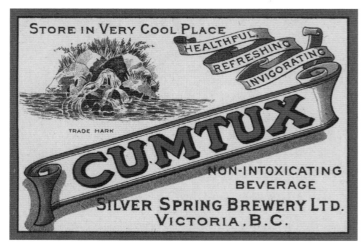

STORE IN VERY COOL PLACE

HEALTHFUL, REFRESHING, INVIGORATING

TRADE MARK

CUMTUX

NON-INTOXICATING BEVERAGE

SILVER SPRING BREWERY LTD. VICTORIA, B.C.

A "near-beer" label. RBCM 989.23.366.

Ale featured a Jack of Hearts playing card glued to the bottle.

Some brewers augmented these colourful brands with audacious claims that their products were "healthful, refreshing and invigorating" and that they contained "backbone" – characteristics that couldn't be advertised today. Invalid Stout took a more subtle approach, playing on the common perception that stout had restorative effects for the sickly.

Keeping pace with public demand was one thing – prohibition was quite another. The long-standing prohibition movement in North America gained significant strength in the years leading up to the First World War. Brewers far and wide found themselves charged with allegations ranging from adulteration of beer to the destruction of families by their association with saloons. Brewers tried to portray beer as a moderate, family drink, but they could not forestall the inevitable.

The First World War provided governments with the opportunity to pass prohibition legislation. The prohibitionists used patriotism to underpin their economic argument of conserving vital resources to win the war – if the boys can give up luxuries overseas, then so must the rest of us. Provincial legislation in October 1917 made it legal for British Columbian saloons to serve only "near beer" – 2.5 proof (about 1.25% alcohol by volume) – which did not impress the drinking public. A person could obtain full-strength alcohol only from a pharmacist after presenting a doctor's prescription. This system was abused, especially around Christmas.

Federal prohibition legislation came into effect in November 1918, which further restricted the local brewing industry by shutting down interprovincial trade in full-strength beer. Victoria entered prohibition with only the Silver Spring and Victoria-Phoenix breweries in operation. Both now had to rely solely on the unpopular "near beer" for domestic sales and on exports to international markets. Any pleas to the governments for compensation for lost revenue fell on deaf ears.

In 1921, the BC government introduced the Moderation Act to combat excessive alcohol use. In a plebiscite held the year before, a majority of the population had voted for this as a viable alternative to outright prohibition. The Moderation Act resulted in the creation of the Liquor Control Board, which became the sole agent for the sale and control of alcohol in the province. Saloons that had survived prohibition by selling "near beer" now closed because they still could not sell full-strength beer by the glass. The public had to purchase beer by the bottle at a government liquor store. One such store that opened at 755 Yates Street on June 15, 1921, saw little business on day one. Many people did not realize that they first needed to buy a permit at a police station. Business would eventually pick up.

In June 1924, after yet another plebiscite, people could buy beer by the glass in licensed premises, though only in electoral districts that voted "wet". Fortunately, for the two local breweries that had survived prohibition, Esquimalt and Royal Oak voted "wet"; the "beer parlours" in those jurisdictions became popular gathering places. Victoria, Saanich

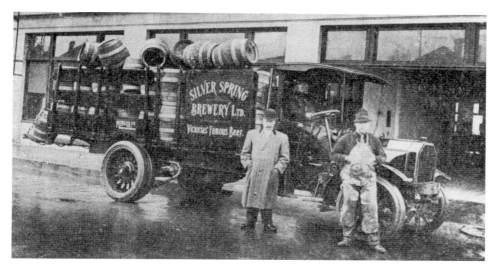

Harry Maynard and a Silver Spring
employee picking up empty kegs from
a customer in downtown Victoria,
about 1913. BC Archives D-07144.

Silver Spring Brewery, 1926. Maynard
and colleagues stand in front of the
brewery's power house. This building
still stands at the corner of Esquimalt
Road and Catherine Street.
Vancouver Public Library 11565.

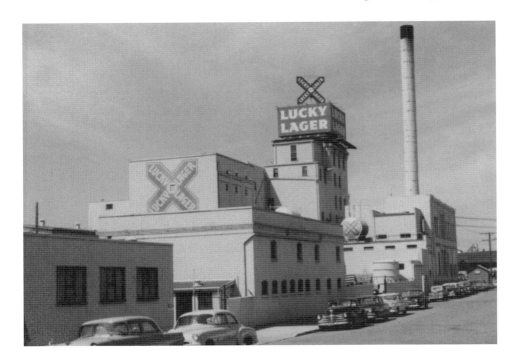

Lucky Lager Brewery at the corner of
Douglas and Discovery streets, 1960s.
Courtesy of Walter Spershott.

BREWED AND BOTTLED IN BRITISH COLUMBIA

ONLY
20¢
MORE PER CASE
THAN BEER

BURTON
TYPE
Ale

Pride of the Pacific

**EQUAL IN QUALITY TO
ANY IMPORTED ALES**

Order Early
for the Holiday Season!

COAST BREWERIES LTD.
Vancouver • New Westminster • Victoria

This advertisement is not published or displayed by the Liquor Control Board or by the Government of British Columbia.

Ad in the *Colonist*, 1947. RBCM.

and Oak Bay remained "dry" until the mid 1950s.
Nevertheless, Silver Spring and Victoria-Phoenix had
regained their local market, though both had built up
a considerable export market in the prohibition years.
By 1925, the Victoria-Phoenix Brewery was exporting
such products as their Export Lager as far as Hong
Kong, Shanghai, Japan and the Dutch East Indies.

In 1928, Robert Fiddes and Associates created
Coast Breweries Ltd in what was then called a strate-
gic alliance. This company held the assets of Victoria-
Phoenix and Silver Spring in Victoria, as well as the
Westminster Brewery in New Westminster and the
Rainier Brewing Company of Canada in Kamloops.
This was not the country's first experience with this
new way of doing business. Breweries had consoli-
dated in Nova Scotia in 1895 and in Quebec just
before the First World War. The die had been cast for
the local industry. In 1934 Coast Breweries took control of General Brewing Corporation of San Francisco
and thereby obtained Lucky Lager.

Ads in the *Colonist*, 1942 (below) and 1948 (right). Courtesy of Greg Evans.

Coast Breweries carried on local brewing for the next 25 years. Gradually, the Silver Spring site did less brewing until it eventually operated as a warehouse. Again, the site maintained its Federal Excise Brewers License with an annual brew there. The Silver Spring brands, such as Silver Spring Bock and Tate's English Ale, became part of the product range being brewed at the Victoria-Phoenix site. The Silver Spring facility was demolished in 1961, with only the brick engine room saved for future use.

In 1954, Coast Breweries became part of Lucky Lager Breweries, with the name officially changing in January 1955. John Labatt Ltd acquired Lucky Lager in 1958 and the brewery in Victoria continued to operate under the name Lucky Lager Brewing Co. (Victoria) Ltd until 1967, when the brewery was given the Labatt's livery and was ultimately closed in 1981 due to company reorganization. It was demolished the following year.

Ad in the *Colonist,* 1936. RBCM.

Flour and Rice Mills

30 bags of flour, shipped by the Grace of God
and in good order.
– Bill of lading from the *Beaver*
(William Brotchie), June 20, 1843

As the Hudson's Bay Company chief factor, James Douglas did not want Fort Victoria to be dependent on imported flour from Oregon. He knew that wheat would have to be to be grown in quantity and that flour mills would be needed to process the grain. As soon as the fort was established, men set about planting grain crops, but four years later the workers were still grinding the wheat with a hand mill, and the fields could not yet produce enough grain to supply the fort, the visiting ships and the other establishments that the fort was expected to provision.

Douglas initiated plans to build a grist mill in 1848. An entry in the Fort Victoria Journal on August 4, 1847, tells of a trip to look at a possible site: "[We ...] proceeded direct for Esquimalt Bay to examine the stream of fresh water ... found it as reported running over a ledge of rock ... well adapted to a mill."

Douglas's January 1848 entry in the journal states: "Mr Nevin and myself started with 8 hands & as many Indians to cut the road to the Mill seat from the plains through the wood to the rapid in Concordia Arm and to bridge that place. I returned in the evening after having marked the route through the woods."

The fort employed eight men to square the timbers for the mill and build a house for mill workers. The countryside about the mill was explored in hopes of finding ground suitable for raising wheat, but "nothing but barriers of rock and swamp" were found in all directions (May 29 journal entry). The machinery did not arrive until March 27, 1850, and when it was finally in place, in July, there was no water. This lack of sufficient water to keep the mill running became the major concern and the great disappointment. Even when the mill had sufficient water it did not have enough grain to meet the demand, so the fort had to continue importing flour.

In a report written to the Hudson's Bay Company in London in 1851, James Douglas explained: "The grain raised in the Colony this year will not be sufficient to meet the home demand, and we shall be under the necessity of making up the deficiency by importing bread stuffs from abroad." A statement of imported provisions for the Fort Victoria Shop recorded 116 barrels of fine flour imported in 1850; in 1853 Douglas bought flour in San Francisco, selling in return a mixed cargo of salmon, cranberries and Nanaimo coal.

In 1855 three flour mills operated in the colony: the HBC's unsuccessful mill at Parson's Bridge, another near the Puget Sound Agricultural Company's Craigflower Farm (see page 14) and John Muir's at Sooke. The steam-powered Craigflower mill went into operation on October 11, 1853, and it was this mill that enabled the Craigflower Farm to establish a successful bakery business. But the mill proved not large enough to meet the bakery's demands, forcing the farm to import flour.

The demand for flour escalated when the miners arrived in 1858. Flour previously selling for $5 a barrel suddenly cost upwards of $15 and sometimes reached the exorbitant price of $30 a barrel. Speculation in flour was of great concern and potentially devastating. One group of enterprising Americans offered to buy the Hudson's Bay Company's entire stock of flour in an attempt to corner the market. But the HBC refused and continued to sell flour at the usual price and in small quantities to individuals only. Another group in the USA tried to deceive buyers by packing flour from Hawaii in bags marked with the stamp of the Golden Gate Company, San Francisco. This company normally supplied high-quality flour, and it must have been a surprise for buyers to find this "Golden Gate" shipment to be dark and full of weevils. Rumours spread that a local firm was also involved in the scheme.

An 1859 report estimated that 3500 barrels of flour on hand would meet the needs of the colony for the next six months. Large quantities of flour were imported from San Francisco, Oregon and the Territory of Washington to meet the demand. The price and availability of flour swung up and down radically, and became a popular subject in newspaper articles. Local merchants tried to keep abreast of the changes and make money when they were able. Speculators seized any opportunity to corner a shipment and increase prices. A delayed ship also meant shortages and higher prices. Merchants had to be astute in their buying. In his book, *The Fraser Mines Vindicated*, Alfred Waddington wrote that

Price of Flour per Barrel	
1858	$5–30
1865	$15–19
1880	$5–7.50
1899	$5–5.50

he believed the California merchants had missed a golden opportunity in 1858 when they failed to see this need for increased supplies of flour: "Not ... a single California merchant thought of sending a single bag of flour to Victoria. The consequence was that shortly after our arrival the bakers were twice short of bread."

The growing population of Victoria read occasional newspaper articles suggesting that a new flour mill would soon be established. In 1860, machinery for two grist mills arrived on the steamer *Golden Hunt*. Reports circulated in 1862 that two Canadians planned to build a steam mill. In 1864 the St George Steam Mill Company proposed to erect a mill in Esquimalt, and two years later a man named Woodcock made a similar proposal. None of these mills came into being. In 1865 the farmers of South Saanich held meetings to consider building a flour mill. A *Colonist* report on August 2, 1867, mentioned that the Spring Ridge Water Company proposed a grist mill, but added that "the only obstacle in the way of the successful working of the mill is the want of water", a problem echoed again and again when local mill sites were considered. Again, these proposals did not go beyond the initial stages.

The local papers frequently published letters to the editor concerning mills. On January 3, 1865, the *Victoria Times* printed a lengthy letter to the editor outlining the need for a flour mill in Victoria and laying out what the writer thought would be the costs of such an operation. The Vancouver Island House of Assembly had passed a resolution that provided a subsidy for the construction of a flour mill that could grind 125 bushels (4400 litres) of wheat a day; it stipulated that 500 bushels of Vancouver Island wheat had to be used before the $1250 subsidy would be paid. The letter writer questioned this requirement, stating that the island could not grow enough wheat to keep the mill busy. Without importing grain, he said, "the mill would stand most unprofitably idle during a greater part of the year".

The first real moves toward establishing flour mills in the Victoria area came in 1867 from beer brewers. In the spring, Laumeister & Gowen announced the opening of a steam flour-milling facility next to their small brewery near Hope Point. With two pairs of grinding stones they could process 100 barrels (11,500 litres) of grain a day. They installed a mechanical tramway to load and unload vessels. Unfortunately, a fire destroyed the mill and the brewery the next year, and Laumeister & Gowen rebuilt only the brewery, a certain financial success.

A small advertisement in the *Colonist* on June 15, 1867, announced the opening of the Colonial Mills on Johnson Street, adjoining the Colonial Brewery, a well-known establishment owned by Arthur Bunster. Bunster had purchased 600 acres (242 hectares) of farm land on the Saanich Peninsula from Thomas Harris. There he grew hops and barley for use in the brewery (see page 84). A slight extension of this business to the farmers made good sense. Bunster advertised that the mill would grind "all kinds of grain on reasonable terms". Other advertisements appeared over the years, each announcing the start-up of the flour mill as farmers brought in the grain harvest. When Arthur Bunster entered politics in 1878, and was elected to Vancouver District, he leased the mill to William Spofford, who changed the name to Victoria Flour Mills.

In that same year, Henry Brackman established his mill in North Saanich. It began as a simple affair in a small building and ended as a large milling company with operations extending across Western Canada. Brackman had emigrated from Germany in 1847, probably landing first in San Francisco and then going to Honolulu where he worked for Harry Rhodes, whose import firm had an outlet in Victoria. Brackman arrived in Victoria in 1862 and made two

Wheat and hay at Dr William Tolmie's Cloverdale Farm, Victoria. Hannah or Richard Maynard photograph. BC Archives F-06701.

trips to the gold fields in BC's interior. The second trip, in 1870, proved successful. When Brackman returned, his first business venture was not milling, but oyster farming at Canoe Cove in partnership with James Brydon, a miller previously employed in Bunster's mill.

In 1878 Brackman built his first mill in North Saanich, on a four-acre (1.6-hectare) site donated for that purpose by pioneer farmer Donald MacDonald. MacDonald had a valid business reason for this generosity. Transporting grain from North Saanich to Victoria was difficult. He wanted a market for the grain grown in the area and to give the farmers a supply of flour and mill by-products (the latter for their cattle). Local farmers supplied wheat, oats, split peas and pearl barley for the mill, and the miller took his payment in a portion of the flour he made. He then shipped the flour to Victoria, Esquimalt and the mainland for sale. Brackman initially went

The original Brackman & Ker Mill at Shoal Bay, Saanich, 1878. Artist unknown; BC Archives I-68508.

into partnership with a Scottish miller named James Milne and they made their first shipment in March 1878. The partnership was dissolved in 1879 and for the next year Brackman operated the mill alone under the name of Saanich Steam Mills. James Brydon replaced Milne as miller, having previously been a miller at Colonial Mills in Victoria. Brydon lived across the bay from the mill, and when Brackman needed him, he signalled Brydon by raising a flag.

Brackman and Brydon ran the mill according to a carefully planned work week. On Monday and Tuesday they dried the oats in a kiln made from a perforated iron plate and fired by wood. On Wednesday they put the oats through hulling stones and fans and then ground the groats on oatmeal stones. They bagged the meal on Thursday and Friday. The Scots living in the neighbourhood claimed that the resulting oatmeal owed its fine flavour to the method of drying and the use of the old-fashioned stones. On Saturday the miller loaded a two-wheeled cart with the bags of oatmeal and hauled it down to the government wharf at Shoal Bay where a Canadian Pacific steamer waited to carry the bags to markets in Victoria and the mainland. Shoal Bay was the only port of call on the Saanich Peninsula with a customs officer, so was the hub of business for North Saanich.

The mill was not the only enterprise undertaken by Brackman. In 1880 he obtained the post-office privilege for North Saanich. Steamers brought the mail several times a week. Brackman also opened a general store in the same building, one of the few stores outside the city at that time. This store remained open after the closing of the flour and oats mill in 1891.

David Russell Ker became associated with Brackman at the Saanich mill in 1880. Ker knew little about milling, so in 1882 he went to San Francisco to gain further experience in the business. On his return in 1883 he became the junior partner in the firm. The capital at the time this partnership was formed was $3200. Ker bought a half interest in the business, paying $350 in cash, the balance to be paid with his half share of the profits. The staff now consisted of Ker, Brydon (the miller) and John Newbigging (an engineer).

Brackman and Ker made the first improvements

Henry Brackman, 1890s.
BC Archives A-02021.

Brackman & Ker offices on Government Street, north of
Johnson Street, 1890s. BC Archives B-04319.

and additions to the mill in 1883. They installed
new machinery that greatly increased the volume of
meal they could produce using the original grinding
stones. They expanded again in 1889 when they built
a second mill in Victoria, a four-storey brick building
worth $11,000 on Wharf Street. Brackman continued
to run the Saanich mill, while Ker ran the Victoria
mill. More space meant more staff and Ker's brothers,
Walter and Thomas, joined the firm.

Brackman and Ker incorporated in 1891 and the
company's capital increased to $150,000. The firm
opened business offices on Government Street, closed
the Saanich mill and announced plans to replace
the Victoria mill with a large new mill on the Outer
Wharf at Ogden Point. The newspaper accounts
waxed eloquent when describing the new $30,000
mill: a modern, five-storey brick building on an
80-by-150-foot lot (24 x 46 metres) ideally situated

on the waterfront where steamers could easily dock;
inside, a 120-horsepower (90-kilowatts) Wheelock
engine ran five pairs of stones for grinding different cereals, and huge bins on the second floor held
grain carried there by an elevator. A *Colonist* story on
January 1, 1893, marvelled at the mill's technology:
"From the time the cereal is transferred [from the
ships] to the dippers of the elevator, there is no more
handling of it except by machinery until it is ready to
be packed in bags and boxes."

Brackman & Ker did considerable advertising, sometimes with other firms, to urge the public
to support local industry, pointing out that all
their grains came from the island or nearby on the
mainland, and that their boxes and bags were made
locally. The annual Agricultural Fair gave the company an opportunity to show its many products.
There, according to a *Colonist* report on October 3,

Two views of National Mills, or the Brackman & Ker
Milling Company, on the Outer Wharf, 1890s. From
Victoria Illustrated 1891 (above) and BC Archives C-08963
(facing page).

1894, Brackman & Ker built "a cosy nook" with a "bower decorated with grain and straw" where staff could "regale the public in real cream and rolled oats". A Victoria Day parade featured its products piled high on a huge wagon drawn by four horses. The company frequently advertised its World's Fair diplomas and medals as evidence of the company's standing in local and foreign markets.

Breakfast cereals became increasingly popular in the 1890s, especially cereals that were easy to prepare. Brackman & Ker made rolled oats and cream of wheat under the National brand name, and a dry cereal called National Wheat Flakes. In 1905 the company launched a contest for the public to select

a name for the Brackman & Ker Nameless Food, a prepared cereal described this way in an August 18 advertisement in the *Colonist*: "It supplies nourishment, strength to the body. Gives vigour and vim to the brain. Adds health, purity to the blood." From the 2,588 entries received, the company selected "Nemo" as the name of the new cereal and paid the winner $25. It also named two other cereals from the contest entries – Pura and Frumetti – and awarded $15 and $10 in prize money respectively.

The Klondike gold rush offered Brackman & Ker an opportunity to supply hundreds of miners with some of the food they required for themselves and their horses. In 1898 the company applied for a

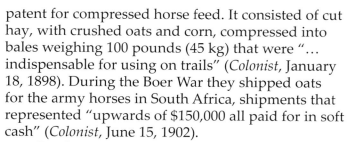

Inside the Brackman & Ker mill, about 1905.
BC Archives B-04112.

Brackman & Ker sacks, 1920s,
RBCM 973.46. 3d, 973.46.5i.

patent for compressed horse feed. It consisted of cut hay, with crushed oats and corn, compressed into bales weighing 100 pounds (45 kg) that were "... indispensable for using on trails" (*Colonist*, January 18, 1898). During the Boer War they shipped oats for the army horses in South Africa, shipments that represented "upwards of $150,000 all paid for in soft cash" (*Colonist*, June 15, 1902).

Brackman & Ker reincorporated in 1899 with capital of $500,000. Then, in 1903, as the firm expanded throughout British Columbia and Alberta, Henry Brackman suddenly died. In 1908, with its capital now at $750,000, the company built a separate plant just for the manufacture of Nemo cereal. It also built new offices and a warehouse, costing $30,000, at the corner of Broad and Pandora streets, and sold the Government Street offices.

In 1909 disaster struck at the mill at the Outer Wharf. One of the millers noticed smoke on the upper floor. As he turned to grab a barrel of water

nearby, the smoke grew into a cloud and the whole floor quickly filled with smoke. The sweeper ran shouting the alarm to the 11 men working on the floor below. The fire spread and gutted the top two floors. A *Colonist* story on October 4 described the result: "the machinery turned into junk piled among charred debris." The fire fighters flooded the lower two floors where the stock was kept. The fire destroyed $15,000 worth of stock, including rose-pattern chinaware premiums intended to be given with National Wheat Flakes. The total loss from the fire was $50,000, but fortunately it was completely covered by insurance.

On June 17, 1910, less than a year after the fire, Brackman & Ker placed a triumphant ad in the *Colonist*: "New Mill Completed: We have erected one of the finest milling plants in Canada, equipped with the very latest and most modern machinery for the production of British Columbia's favourite breakfast food." The firm continued to grow with the purchase

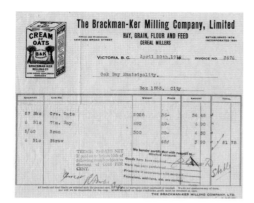

Invoice from 1912. RBCM 980.79.2g.

Western Canada Flour Mills, Brackman & Ker, 1910s.
BC Archives I-68533.

of the Western Milling Company in Calgary in 1912; in 1913 it amalgamated with Western Canada Flour Mills, a mill known for its Purity brand flour. The company closed and dismantled the Victoria mill in 1928.

Not every mill began as a flour mill. Rice regularly arrived in the port of Victoria from China as a return cargo for exports of lumber, coal and even cranberries. This rough rice needed milling to produce clean rice, rice meal, rice flour and rice starch. Some rice mills later converted into flour mills.

One successful example of this was the Victoria Roller Flour and Rice Mill (or Victoria Rice Mill). In 1886 the Mount Royal Milling & Manufacturing Company of Montreal established a rice mill on Store Street, with Thomas Hall of Hall, Ross & Company as manager. Their intention was to build an adjoining flour mill, but they never did. Mount Royal saw that it was more economical to supply rice to places west of Winnipeg from Victoria rather than to ship it through the Suez Canal and across the Atlantic to Montreal. The stone buildings on the property

had originally been owned by Dickson, Campbell & Company. To these buildings Mount Royal added two storeys, a boiler and an engine house to the back of the building. Described by the *Colonist* (January 1, 1886) as "a comparatively small mill", the Victoria Rice Mill had the most modern machinery available along with a large, convenient wharf where ocean vessels could unload their cargo.

In 1889 the Victoria Rice Mill bought the *Thermopylae*, a tea clipper, from the Aberdeen White Star Line, and for six years it was the only ship registered in the port of Victoria. Repainted white and converted to a barque, the *Thermopylae* carried cargoes of lumber from Puget Sound and British Columbia to China, then returned with rice for the Victoria mill. The ship carried an armament of two cannons and 24 rifles along with cutlasses and boarding pikes as defence against pirates along the Chinese coast. By 1895 it was obvious that steamships were more efficient and the upkeep of the aging vessel was greater than the profits. The *Thermopylae* was sold to the Portuguese to be used as a naval training vessel.

Victoria Roller Flour and Rice Mill on Store Street, 1891–92. BC Archives G-02970.

The rear of same mill, in the 1880s. Hannah or Richard Maynard photograph; BC Archives D-05995.

In 1890 the city passed Rice Mill and Flour Mill Bonus bylaws, offering an exemption from municipal taxes and free water for 15 years to Victoria mills as an incentive to expand. Victoria Rice Mill took advantage, adding a flour mill to the business. The company planned to ship flour to China on the *Thermopylae.* The city gave $10,000 to the Victoria Rice Mill to help it establishment of the flour mill, but on condition that no Chinese were to be employed. The efforts of the company to establish a profitable mill came to nothing when new tariffs on rice made it impossible continue. The mill closed in 1897.

"Old Rice Mills to be Re-opened" announced the *Colonist* on June 2, 1907: "the refitting of the old rice mills on Store Street is almost complete". The article went on to say that the company hoped to process 10 tons of rice per day in the beginning and increase to 40 tons per day. If the mills ran at night, they felt they could double the capacity. A flour mill was to be started later. But the future of the company did not run according to plan. In 1908 the city withdrew an annual operating subsidy and the company declared bankruptcy.

The large mills produced most of the rice flour for use in the city, but the Chinese community also had a thriving parallel industry. At least eight small rice mills operated in Victoria in the 1890s, all owned and operated by Chinese. Gan Fook Yuen operated three steam-powered mills in his building on Government Street. Other mills worked simply by manually raising large stone hammers with cams and allowing them to fall under their own weight onto the rice held in hollowed-out stone containers.

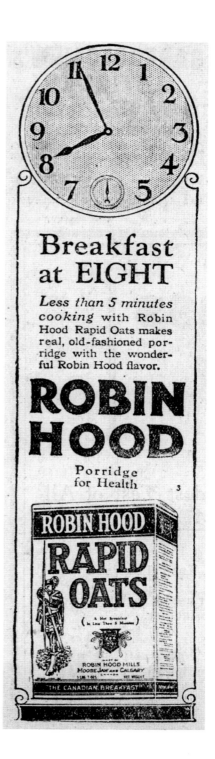

Ads in the *Colonist* on August 28, 1938 (above), and
January 27, 1926 (right).

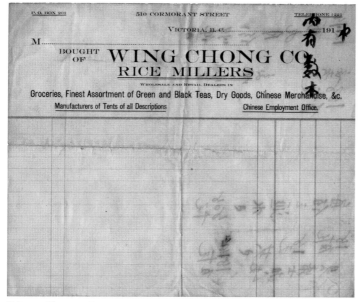

Wing Chong Company invoice.
RBCM 966.87.86.

Ad in the *Colonist* on March 2, 1928.

Preserving Food

Tues. Sept. 12, 1893. Met Ben Stone on Johnson Street. He gave me a salted salmon…. Went to the Board of Trade Rooms … to hear members … consider the Cold Storage business.
    – Alexander MacMillan, from his diary.

In Victoria's early days, people preserved food by salting, smoking or canning it, or by keeping it cold with blocks of ice. Governor James Douglas promoted an unsuccessful scheme to bring ice from Sitka for local use and trade. But the cold winters of the mid 1800s meant that ice could be cut from the rivers and ponds around Victoria and on the mainland. Blocks of ice cut from the lakes and rivers in the winter were stored in sawdust for use later in the year. Companies on the mainland supplied ice from Fort Hope and the Fraser River. Swan Lake was a good local source of ice, and an icehouse was built on the shore. In 1865, J.B. Sere of Mount Tolmie harvested ice from a pond on his property. Alexander Phillips advertised that he would deliver ice anywhere in town; he focused on supplying hotels, restaurants and saloons. Ice suppliers charged 5 to 15 cents a pound. These prices led a shop owner to announce that he would stop selling ice cream, because 10 cents a pound for ice was too expensive. This was a great disappointment to the townspeople, who appreciated his ice cream in the warm summer months.

Refrigeration reduced the necessity to harvest ice. By 1895 the BC Storage and Ice Works was manufacturing ice from distilled water and providing 100,000 square feet (9300 square metres) of cold-storage space for perishable food.

BC Storage and Ice Works used the romance of the Klondike as a theme for their float in the 1900 Victoria Day parade, as described in the *Colonist* on May 25, 1900:

A scene from the Klondike followed a float arranged by the ice company. Huge blocks of ice were surmounted by a Klondike sleigh in which were seated a little boy and girl muffled up to the ears in furs. The effect was very pretty.

Blocks of ice can preserve food for only a short time, so people developed other methods of preventing spoilage. Salt was good for preserving meat, fish and butter.

The residents of Fort Victoria ate fresh fish and meat when they could get it, but one of the mainstays of the fort diet was salted salmon. Local First Peoples brought fresh salmon and herring in season to trade at the fort. Out of season, the fort relied on supplies of salted salmon from Fort Langley and Fort Vancouver. Barrels of salmon arrived annually from Fort Vancouver in transit to other forts up the coast. Some remained in the Fort Victoria stores for their own use. Chief Factor Roderick Finlayson

J.B. Sere of Mount Tolmie harvested ice from his pond to sell in Victoria. BC Archives H-00789.

At home, people could preserve eggs in a form of gelatine called isinglass or water glass. To make the preservative, mix one part isinglass with nine parts water, cover the eggs entirely with the solution, put weight (e.g., a plate) on the eggs to keep them from floating, and store in a cool place.

estimated that Fort Victoria required 100 barrels (11,500 litres) of salted salmon to last through the non-summer months. In October 1844, he wrote to John McLaughlin in Fort Vancouver:

> Notwithstanding every encouragement being held out to the natives to bring salmon for trade, we have only been able to procure 30 barrels of which 10 still remain and will not last us longer than the end of this month.

The solution was to build a salmon-curing house in Victoria. McLaughlin had sent specific instructions to Finlayson on this matter in March 1844. The curing house should also have a storage facility for loading ships with salted salmon for up-coast destinations. The stores should be able to hold 600 to 800 barrels (70,000 to 93,000 litres) of salmon and 200 to 300 bushels (7,000 to 10,000 litres) of salt. McLaughlin even recommended where to build it:

> The best place appears to be Steamers' Wharf, where vessels can lay in 3 fm [fathoms (5.5 metres)] water with their sides touching the rocks and goods can be landed and reshipped with very little labour. The stores ought to be

large, substantially built of rough wood, and covered with 36-inch [90-cm] shingle."

In June 1855 Finlayson reported that the salmon store had been built, as ordered, along similar lines to the barns east of the fort. The building measured 30 by 6 metres with a 2.75-metre ceiling. A two-metre-wide door in the middle of the building led to a wooden wharf where the barrels could be landed and loaded with ease.

The salmon house served a variety of functions. Wells, Fargo & Company had an office in one corner until they built their own on Yates Street. Another corner provided "hotel accommodation" of a most rustic sort for $2 a night. Naval officers even staged a ball there, as reported by Michael Kluckner in his book, *Victoria: The Way It Was*). The officer in charge of the event wrote:

> It was a most dismal-looking place, enough to drive all thoughts of dancing out of one's head. We got all the flags we could from the ship and turned in 30 or 40 sailors and in a short time a fairy palace of flags was erected, so that not a particle of the building was visible; we then

Pacific Sauce and Vinegar Works, 1890s. Hannah Maynard photograph; BC Archives A-04651.

Prices of Preserved Meat

| 1858 | corned beef | 7¢ per lb |
| 1878 | salted salmon | 12½¢ per lb |

rigged up some large chandeliers and sconces of bayonets and ramrods wreathed in evergreens which when lighted up produced a regular blaze of light and made quite a fairy scene. In this transformed atmosphere, a supper for 200 people was served. After the fort buildings and palisade were torn down, the salmon house remained and it became a theatre.

Salted salmon – or any salted meat – had to be prepared carefully and the brine had to be replaced periodically. Meanwhile, as the town grew, small businesses set themselves up to cure fish. The 1862 city directory lists Phineas Manson & Company as fish curers. They delivered their preserved fish to W.B. Smith's grocery on Government Street. Other fish curers were on Humboldt Street, Waddington Alley, Yates Street and Oriental Alley. Hah Choo appeared in the directory in 1869 as a fish curer on Cormorant Street.

Compared with the lengthy process of preserving meat and fish, the preparation of fruit was easy. Wild fruits and, before long, cultivated fruits were readily available around the fort. Housewives made jams and jellies. Those who did not prepare their own could buy products from England in the stores. The earliest advertisement for preserved fruit made from local produce appeared in the *Colonist* on December 7, 1860: Madame Lacharme "respectfully [invites] the Ladies of Victoria and the general public to pay a visit to the Colonial Market and inspect her preserves of every description, vegetables, fruits and marmalades", all produced on Vancouver Island. In 1882, the British Columbia Directory pointed out:

All descriptions of fruit come to perfection. There is no reason why the canning of apples, pears, peaches, plums, nectarines, apricots, etc., should not in the course of time become one of the most remunerative of the local industries.

Preserving factories did, indeed, become a local industry in the late 1880s and remained active until the years prior to the Second World War, when amalgamation reduced their number.

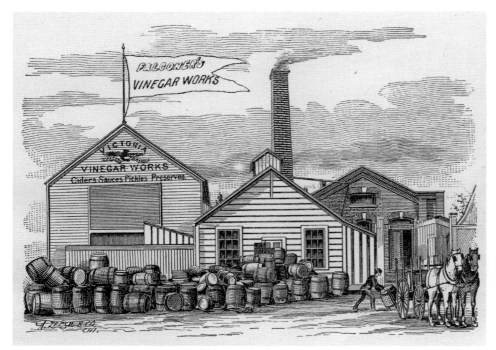

From *Victoria Illustrated* 1891.

J.H. Falconer, 1920. Steffens-Colmer photograph; BC Archives G-08544.

These factories produced fruit and vegetable preserves, fruit syrups, ketchups, vinegars, jams, mincemeats, pickles, ciders and flavouring extracts. They packaged them in glass jars, tins, wooden pails and tubs. H.G. Brady & Company, established in 1885, was also known as the Pacific Sauce and Vinegar Works. It was listed at 183 Johnson Street in 1895, but moved to 66-68 Blanshard Street in 1899. In 1906, the *Colonist* reported that the company employed four men and two boys continuously during the year and had an annual payroll of $3000. The company purchased all its raw materials from market farms and gardens in Victoria and north on Vancouver Island.

In April 1891 James Falconer arrived from Toronto and established a cider and pickling factory at 155-157 Yates Street. He had previously worked in this trade in Glasgow and London. An engraving from the period shows a small wooden building that had been damaged in a fire caused by a defective chimney and furnace in June, August and September of 1892. The loss in these three fires amounted to $20. The firm carried no insurance. On December 28, Falconer placed an advertisement in the *Colonist* asking for a factory site of "two full lots about seven blocks from the Post Office, for two factories to employ about 50 hands; one factory to be built within two months." He asked any property owner who held waterfront privileges to contact him. The land obtained, Falconer built a factory at 126-128 Fort Street. He made a wide range of preserves using local fruits and vegetables. He imported Ontario cider and Quebec maple syrup and produced large quantities of sauerkraut for use by the sealing fleet. In his large displays at the Agricultural Fair he showed his many medals, diplomas and letters from distinguished officials as evidence of his superior products.

Falconer was an ambitious businessman and interested in becoming involved in the community. Within a year of coming to Victoria he was on the board of the BC Agricultural Fair. Two years later he was in Kamloops where he proposed a fruit and vegetable cannery. He argued that the local farmers would find it to their advantage to grow the produce required in large quantities. The *City News* of Dawson City places him in that town in 1900, where he had purchased mineral springs on Bonanza Creek and was planning to erect a bottling works and hotel. He planned to purchase the furnishings and fittings for the hotel in Victoria. In 1901, when the Dawson City council proposed that the municipality own and operate a brewery, James Falconer served on the committee. On January 10, Dawson's *Daily Klondike Nugget* observed, "J.H. Falconer, late of Bennett, says he always makes a speech when the opportunity presents."

In 1891 Samuel M. O'Kell arrived in Victoria, like Falconer, to look for a location for a preserving factory. His boyhood friend, Walter Morris, arrived soon after. They had been partners in the preserving business in Bolton and Manchester, England. The O'Kell & Morris Preserving Company established a factory in Rock Bay. The company quickly turned its attention to marketing opportunities outside British Columbia, in Winnipeg and England. It produced whole-fruit preserves, jams, jellies and marmalades – all from locally grown fruit – in glass containers and shipped them by the carload to eastern markets. The company's advertisements frequently included "Encourage Home Industry", a slogan used by many firms in the city, and gave four reasons for Victorians to support O'Kell & Morris: it employed local labour, it bought high-quality local fruit, it used BC sugar and it used packages manufactured in BC. In 1895 its line of products consisted of fruit jams and jellies,

> Sound the loud timbre!
> O'er Canada's fair land
> For fine marmalades, jams and jellies
> Go to Falconer's stand.
> – *Colonist* ad, February 9, 1895.

candies, fruit peel, mincemeat, and all kinds of canned fruit. Later it added pickles to the list.

Walter Morris resigned as manager of the company in 1894 and turned his attention to the salmon canning industry. O'Kell continued in the preserving business and brought W.H. Price to town to work for him. According to an ad in the *Colonist* on October 4, Price had "obtained the gold medal as jam boiler against the world". (He later left the firm and formed Price Preserving Company in Esquimalt.) O'Kell's advertisements now included references to various medals and testimonials from such important figures as Lord Aberdeen and the Governor General of Canada. Even the mincemeat held a pedigree, being "the Queen's Mincemeat, made from the recipe of the Queen's chef" (*Colonist*, December 24, 1897). As a further reminder of the company's success, it adopted the brand name "Gold Medal".

A smaller firm, Le Vatte & Ward Cider and Sauce Company, began doing business in 1895. On September 2, the *Colonist* proclaimed that this new company had "a first class article in their line" and that its sauce "conceded to have no equal in the Dominion".

RBCM 990.52.3z.

Product label. RBCM 990.52.3w.

Vinegar bottles from Western Pickling Works, Victoria, and Spencer's, Vancouver. RBCM 987.114.17, 973.169.100.

In 1906 F.R. Stewart & Company, produce brokers, entered the jam-making business. Its factory on lower Yates Street employed 15 men and had an annual payroll of $8500. It used only local fruit and sold jams under the brand names "Diadem" and "Crown".

Local growers supplied most of the produce for the preserving factories, and they needed labourers to help harvest their crops. Berry farmers hired pickers from First Nations and Asian populations and a pool of casual Caucasian labourers. In 1881 fruit growers in the United States developed loganberries, a hybrid of blackberries and raspberries, and farmers around Victoria welcomed this new berry, which produced abundantly and met a ready market. Loganberries not only made fine jams and firm canned fruit, but also a palatable wine.

To meet the demand for loganberry preserves, several new companies got into the market and sold their products locally, across Canada and to England. The berries that these companies did not process appeared in local groceries and fruit stands. Advertisements encouraged housewives to buy their supply of fruit for preserving before the factories began processing and supplies became limited.

J.J. White started the Saanich Canning Company in 1905, after he saw First Peoples gathering clams and selling them across the United States border. He set up a cannery next to his general store and began canning the clams in their own juices (see page 151). Later, the company began canning berries as well. At peak season Saanich Canning employed more than 100 people. Its advertisements emphasized that it was a local company using local materials: "87% goes into wages, printing, raw material, etc. Your money stays at home. You support us. We support others." The company shipped its products nationwide and overseas. BC Packers bought it in 1939.

Berry pickers. Victoria City Archives PR263-282 M08198.

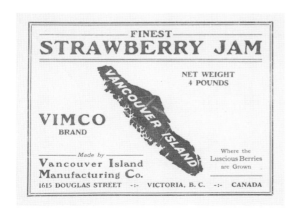

RBCM 990.52.3x.

RBCM 982.19.4.

A tomato crop near Victoria, 1926. BC Archives I-52284.

RBCM 990.52.3y.

Growers Wine Company started in Victoria in 1922. Slinger's was its leading brand. The winery closed in 1977. RBCM 2000.33.55.

A variety of canned goods began to appear in Victoria in the late 19th century. Canned salmon, tomatoes, corn and beans became widely available in the 1870s. Wholesalers and producers brought a multitude of other products from the mainland: crystallized, evaporated and glacé fruits; dried, salted or canned meats; and canned and dried vegetables.

The consumption of canned food and preserves increased in the early 20th century, and new companies arose to fill the demand. The Sidney Canning Company processed fish until business declined after the First World War and the plant ended its days rendering dogfish for fertilizer and other oil products. Todd & Sons also operated a fish cannery in Esquimalt. Gordon Head Canning operated from 1932 to 1948, canning "fruits, vegetables, and other products of the soil". During the 1920s and '30s Holsum Packing, which became Victoria Fruit Packing Company in 1937, operated a cannery at Lake Hill. Beach-Eakins, a company based in Mission on the mainland, operated a plant in Victoria, as did the Cedar Hill Canning Company. But local canners had difficulty competing with imported products.

Only Saanich Canning and Holsum Packing appear to have enjoyed much success.

In the 1930s the B. Wilson Company introduced frozen foods to Victoria, which by the 1950s replaced many of the canned goods on store shelves. This ice-making company patented a process it called "frosting": it cooled fruits and vegetables down to zero or slightly below as quickly as possible and packaged them in wax paper. The package could be held for 24 hours before use. In 1939, B. Wilson advertised a 12-ounce box of "garden-fresh" peas for 19 cents. Instructions on the boxes of frozen vegetables advised the consumer to boil peas or asparagus for 10 minutes and lima beans for 25 minutes (rather long by today's standards), with a caution against overcooking.

B. Wilson workers preparing fruit for freezing, 1947.
Duncan MacPhail photograph; BC Archives, I-01835.

RBCM 990.52.3t.

Wholesale Merchants

Economy in working a business here is everything, and I have always looked upon this as
the chief consideration in our arrangements
here.

    – Robert Rithet letter to Gilbert Sproat
     in San Francisco, 1868

In the late 1850s the commercial merchants' wooden houses crowded both sides of Wharf Street, which the *Colonist* on December 18, 1858, labelled an "impassable" street, so muddy that "Myer's Wharf cannot be reached". Wharves extended along the harbour where ships from London, Hawaii, the USA and Russia disgorged their cargo. Gradually the frame buildings gave way to brick warehouses. It was one of these buildings, built by James Wilcox in 1859, that boasted a cast iron front on the ground floor – the first of its kind in Victoria. Some of the warehouses on the water side of the street were built on piles. This allowed thieves to break into one of these warehouses by cutting a hole in the floor and then lower the goods into a boat during low tide.

Victoria's import-export trade expanded rapidly in 1858 in response to the needs of the thousands of miners arriving from San Francisco and eastern Canada and the United States. With the miners came merchants eager to make their money not in the rigours of the gold fields, but in the commerce associated with the influx of miners. Charles Evans, who worked as a commission agent from 1862 to 1863, described his arrival in 1862:

> Arrived at Esquimalt about 1 o'clock a.m. Came ashore about 4 o'clock, shouldered our dunnage and marched to Victoria, about 4 miles. Bought some bread, bacon, etc. and pitched our tent outside the corporation.... Slept in our tent for the first time.

Evans was one of the men who came to Victoria, set up a business (Beaven & Evans, General Agents) and then left for other pursuits in quick order. Others, such as Robert Rithet, began businesses that lasted well into the 20th century and were continued by their sons.

Merchant houses imported and exported all kinds of preserved foods, fresh produce, meat, hardware and clothing. They acted as storage agents, money exchangers and gold agents. They held and forwarded mail, and stored miners' belongings until they came back from the gold fields (if they did). The merchants themselves had strong links with San Francisco, moving freely between the two cities and frequently operating in both countries; for some the Victoria operation was a branch of a company based in San Francisco.

Merchants eagerly awaited the arrival of a supply ship. A man posted on Beacon Hill watched for the first appearance of a sail. He then rode quickly to Esquimalt Harbour to supervise the unloading, for

Looking north on Wharf Street from Fort Street, about 1864. Richard Carr's wholesale business is four doors north. The Hudson's Bay Company warehouse is across the street, and Edgar & Aimé is on the next block. BC Archives A-03033.

SS *Amelia* and SS *Olympian* at the wharves of Turner,
Beeton & Company, 1890s. BC Archives D-09332.

time was money and the freight still had to be moved
to Victoria. As early as 1859, businessmen argued for
the dredging of the harbour in Victoria so that ships
might anchor there. Some dredging began in 1866.

The cargos that landed at the wharves contained
a broad assortment of goods, from living animals and
fresh produce to preserved food. In the early days the
newspapers detailed the cargo on each ship, listing,
in addition, any passengers who might be aboard.
Shipments from Honolulu contained not only the
expected sugar and molasses, but ducks, oranges,
peanuts, watermelons, corn, coconuts and poi. These
cargos offered the population relief from a plain diet;
Victoria's Hawaiian community must have been
delighted with the arrival of a shipment of poi. In
1861 *The Victoria Press* reported imports for the year
to be worth over $2.5 million.

But this flow of goods could be delayed by bad
weather or American embargos, or interrupted by the
loss of ships that carried thousands of dollars worth
of produce. A ship gone down with its cargo could

be financially ruinous to any merchant house that
had invested in the cargo. In a letter written in 1860,
commercial merchants Edgar & Aimé feared the
worst: "The *Vickers* has not arrived and the general
impression is that she has been lost…. One of the
big merchants looks somewhat blue as they have
quite a number of goods on her and we are told no
insurance." The *Vickers* had indeed sunk with $13,623
worth of goods on her, some of it for the grocer,
William B. Smith.

The early commercial-merchant firms in Victoria
were small and often short-lived. The letter book of
Edgar & Aimé for September 1860 to October 1862
reveals the business dealings of one of these small
firms. Edgar & Aimé conducted its business in a
frame building on Wharf Street. The letters record
not only the company's business dealings but also
local gossip, and the occasional reference to business
intrigues. No records have been found to indicate
when the company was established, but it must have
been during the early gold rush to serve the incoming

Rithet's Pier on Huron Street, Victoria, about 1890.
BC Archives B-02694.

miners. Business was difficult and the letter book suggests that Edgar & Aimé thought that many of the new commercial houses would soon disappear: "We think some of them will get sick of it before the season is over." D.A. Edgar was probably an American. He seemed to have close ties to commercial houses in San Francisco and to the eastern USA. The other partner, Aimé Guilloteau was French.

Edgar & Aimé's main imports were flour and produce, but nothing was too big (a complete stove with boiler) or too small (a letter) for the firm to handle. Eggs arrived by steamer, sometimes in good order, sometimes scrambled, frequently rotten. Chickens came in crates; if the order was short, it was assumed that some of the birds had died during the passage. The company also imported trees, grass seed, fruit, vegetables, sugar and baking powder. One consignment of butter had been packed in used tobacco cans, which spoiled the taste.

The firm also sent goods out, to New Westminster and on to the gold fields during the open season. It attempted exporting goods to San Francisco. An order of cranberries, sent to Royal Fisk & Company to be sold in San Francisco, was something of a disappointment to the company. Packed in barrels filled with water, the cranberries were expected to keep for about a year. Edgar & Aimé intended them for the California mines, but the berries failed to sell. Letter after letter asked about their fate, each time suggesting a lower price; then finally, "Make the loss and have done with it."

Edgar & Aimé kept a sharp eye out for new opportunities. When the American Desiccating Company of New York began manufacturing dried meats and vegetables, Edgar & Aimé seized upon the idea. Dried foods were compact and light, easier and less expensive to ship north and to the mainland. Although some called these new products "Yankee

Oppenheimer Bros mercantile store in Yale, 1868. Edgar & Aimé conducted business with this merchant. Richard Maynard photograph; BC Archives E-01924.

humbug", Edgar & Aimé hoped to make a consider-able profits on their sale. "We shall spare no pain or expense in trying to introduce them." The dried food was packed in 10-pound tins and labelled with a recipe on the side. Edgar & Aimé added more instructions:

> If you take a piece of the Beef Soup 1 inch square and let it soak for a short time and then boil it you will find that you have enough soup for two or three men. If you add a little Water to the Potatoes and let them soak you will find they increase very much and all they need is a little boiling to make them the same as potatoes, which they are, compressed.

The firm also ordered cases of desiccated mixed vegetables, beef hash and beef soups costing between 30 and 50 cents a pound. But sales were slow. In 1862, Edgar & Aimé reported to Royal Fisk & Company, San Francisco: "We have not sold much this season but hope to next and if we can introduce them we think they will sell well."

The keeping of the books must have been dif-ficult. Payment was made to the firm in British pounds sterling, American eagles, sovereigns, gold bars or gold dust. The gold bars and dust were not always well marked. "Be a little more careful," Edgar & Aimé wrote to a client in Douglas (on the mainland), "have the packages of Dust marked as the last one lay in the office for some days before it was delivered." Northern clients did not always pay their bills promptly, and neither did Edgar & Aimé. Many letters request that money owed be sent immediately. Others explain to their American connections that the money will be sent on the next steamer to San Francisco. The amount of credit extended to the mer-chants in BC's interior was considerable. One firm in Douglas was urged to at least reduce their debt to $10,000.

Supplies came not only from San Francisco but also from Oregon and the Territory of Washington. The letters indicate that Edgar & Aimé shipped goods to merchants in New Westminster and in towns in

John Wilkie & Company's premises at the corner of Wharf Street and Bastion Square, about 1864. Among goods imported and offered for sale in 1864 were 160 bags of coffee direct from Cost Rica. BC Archives B-02227.

Edgar and Aimé were not shy about giving fatherly advice. In a letter to a New Westminster firm that was in their debt they wrote:

> We are sorry to hear you want an extension to the amount of your indebtedness. We are willing to grant your request. And at the same time would state that in our opinion had both remained at New Westminster and attended to your business instead of sporting around Victoria the past Winter you would not be in the position you are in now.

R.P. Rithet staff in the office, 1912. BC Archives H-04040.

Rithet's warehouse on Pier No. 2, 1930.
BC Archives D-01658.

Native of the Tropics:
While some bananas were being
unpacked at F.R. Stewart ... a monster adder fell on the floor.... They
have presented it to the Provincial
Museum.
    – *Colonist*, October 26, 1899.

1919 ad. RBCM 2000.33.59.

Robert Patterson Rithet, about 1880.
John Savannah photograph;
BC Archives G-07665.

Richard Carr, about 1876.
BC Archives E-09910.

BC's interior. All shipments depended on the arrival of steamers and the roads in the interior being open. Winter was a slow time and "business was dull", particularly when the weather was "cold enough to freeze the balls off a Brass Monkey."

In March 1861, with much excitement, Edgar wrote to Royal Fisk & Company: "We expect to move into a Brick Building in a few months." This would have been a great step upward, for brick buildings were much sought after in the sea of wood-frame buildings. But by December the plans had been modified. "We are moving into Geo. Reynolds' old building opposite on Wharf [across the street].... We cannot stand the press to pay $125 per month for a Brick Building yet awhile." In January 1862 the new premises was "set right" and business continued as before. But on July 12, the *Victoria Chronicle* described the doubtful stature of the warehouse: "The building

presents the appearance of a stove pipe hat with all the stiffening removed." Sure enough, disaster struck the wood-frame warehouse one night in September 1863 when the floor, heavily weighted with goods, collapsed upon the beer barrels stored below in the basement. The firm moved back to their "old stand" across the street while repairs were made.

The business license assessment rolls in 1862 listed the value of Edgar & Aimé at £4000, well below the assessed value of the Hudson's Bay Company, but still a respectable position compared with other merchants in Victoria. Letters in late 1862 begin to mention "squaring away" with Royal Fisk & Company and paying all debts to other firms in San Francisco, and urging some of the company's creditors in BC to quickly pay what they owed. A letter to P. Smith & Company in Pemberton reminded the owner that he owed at least $2000. Another, in

October, complains: "Trade here is now very dull and the large amount of Foreign goods [that] keeps pouring in plays the D-----l [devil] with things."

In 1866 Edgar & Aimé was assessed at $1000, placing it well below grocers James Fell and Carlos Bossi, baker Samuel Nesbitt, and butcher Fred Reynolds. It is not clear whether the business was failing or one of the partners decided to dissolve the partnership. Either way, Edgar & Aimé became D.A. Edgar & Company and in 1867 no longer appeared in the city directory. The assessment rolls indicated an its value at "$000". Aimé Gouilloteau also continued to be listed as a merchant on Wharf Street until 1867.

Edgar & Aimé was a small and short-lived commission agent among those that dotted wharf street. Robert Patterson Rithet was one of the more prominent agents. Arriving in Victoria in 1861 Rithet established a wholesale grocery business and from this basis became involved in many business enterprises, including the construction of the outer docks and several fish canneries. Commission agents Robert C. Janion, Goodwin & Company and Richard Carr (father of the famous painter and writer, Emily Carr) also had offices and warehouses on Wharf Street.

Richard Carr carried out a wholesale business in a brick warehouse on Wharf Street across from the Hudson's Bay Company warehouse from the late 1850s until his death in 1888. In *The Book of Small* (1942), Emily Carr, remembers her father's store:

> The inside of Father's store was deep and dark. Cases, crates and barrels stood piled one on top of another right up to the ceiling, with just a narrow lane running down the middle and ending in what was called "the yard" – not a yard at all, only a strong, rough board shed filled with "empties".... There were no windows.... Slits of daylight cut between the boards of the shed walls, and the shadows thrown by a sputtering gas jet made it all spooky and unreal – different from the solid, comfortable feel of the outer store crammed with provisions....

R.C. Janion's store on Wharf Street, 1880s.
BC Archives A-05554.

Kwong Lee & Company on Cormorant Street, which has been decorated for the 1876 visit of Lord Dufferin, Governor General of Canada. BC Archives E-01926.

Father's office was beside the open front of his big store, and in it Father sat in front of a large, square table covered with green baize: on it in front of him was a cupboard full of drawers and pigeon-holes. He sat in a high-backed wicker armchair.... A fat round stove, nearly always hot, was between Father's table and the long, high desk where his men stood or sat on high stools doing their books when they were not trundling boxes on a truck. There was an iron safe in one corner of the office with a letter press on top and there were two yellow chairs for customers to sit on while Father wrote their orders in his book. Everything was dozened in Father's store; his was not a business that sold things by pinches in paper bags. High along the wall ran four long shelves, holding glass jars of sample English sweets – all pure, all wholesome, all English. The labels said so.

Chinese merchants had shops along Cormorant (now Pandora) Street, some of them large import-export firms with offices in San Francisco. These firms came in 1858 with the purpose of contracting labour and selling supplies to the gold mines. They built stores and warehouses and began investing in real estate. A *Colonist* article on January 1, 1884, reported that the Chinese import houses of Tai Wo, Ching Kee & Company, Kwong Lee & Company, Kwong Chung & Company, Tai Ching Yuen and Tai Yuen Lung Kee all expected a considerable increase in trade. It went on to say that these firms planned to erect more buildings and import eastern fruit via the soon-to-be completed Canadian Pacific Railway.

One of the most successful of the Chinese firms was Kwong Lee & Company, owned by two brothers, Loo Chuck Fan and Loo Chew Fan. An advertisement in the *Colonist* on May 15, 1860, listed 3000 mats of No. 1 Chinese rice, 500 gallons (2300 litres) of Chinese oil and 50 packages of "first quality" tea to be auctioned by the prominent auctioneer Phillip M. Backus on Yates Street.

Public Markets

There is no country in the world where farmers more richly deserve encouragement than on Vancouver Island … vote "aye" for a public market.
— *Colonist* editorial, January 5, 1887

As the colony grew, so to did the problem of getting food to those who needed it. The Chinese farmers put their produce into baskets slung on each end of a long pole and moved around the neighbourhoods at what other colonists described as a jog. The European farmers placed their produce into wagons and took it to the local grocers or sold it door to door. At the end of the day the unsold fruit and vegetables had to be disposed of at a reduced price or taken back to the farm to be used as food for the animals, a rather unsatisfactory end to a long day. Time spent peddling produce was time spent away from farming. It became obvious that the town needed a weekly public market similar to those people had known in other parts of the world.

At Craigflower Farm the Puget Sound Agricultural Company decided that there were enough independent settlers in the area to support a public market, so in 1856 it started a monthly market, but this was local and did not supply the town of Victoria.

On November 21, 1860, a *Colonist* editorial announced: "The Hudson's Bay Company, in a moment of generous aberration, has determined to present the town with a piece of land adjoining the fort for the purpose of a market." But this did not happen. The next year, some private citizens saw an entrepreneurial opportunity and formed the Victoria Market Company. This prompted a flurry of letters to newspaper editors protesting the new company, for now the profits from the market would go to private speculators rather than the town coffers. On June 23, one letter writer in the *Colonist* lamented, "What has become of the lot promised by Mr Dallas before leaving Victoria and previous to the sale of the fort property?"

The Victoria Market Company directors were Kenneth McKenzie (chairman), J.J. Cochrane (secretary-treasurer), T.J. Skinner, Robert Burnaby, Alex Munro, G.T. Gordon, Alexander Watson and Robert Ker. They acquired land bounded by Broad, Broughton, Douglas and Fort streets. The company's viability was based on the sale of 80 shares at $100 each and the projection that a minimum of 12 stalls would be rented at $10 per month. To this was to be added rent from two cottages on Fort Street and from other outbuildings on the property.

The building of the market began in July 1861 and the daily papers followed its progress with great interest. Four wood-frame buildings were removed and a brick building, described as "large … and most commodious", rose at the corner of Broad and Fort,

Charges at the Victoria Market

Stalls per month $10.00
Stalls per day $0.75
Stand for produce cart in yard per month $7.50
Stand for produce cart in yard per day $0.50

No entrance fee charged for carts bringing in produce
for sale at stalls.

H. Henley, Clover Point Gardens, respectfully informs the inhabitants of Victoria that he has taken a STALL IN THE NEW MARKET for the sale of Fruit trees, Seeds, Vegetables and Flowering Plants of many kinds, Herb plants and, in short, all kinds of garden produce. Gardens neatly laid out. Two hundred thousand Cabbage Plants of eight varieties for sale.
– *Victoria Press*, October 10, 1861.

at a reported cost of $6000. A market keeper was chosen from some 60 applicants at a salary of $60 per month. In mid September the market opened. It was a simple opening, with "a public demonstration … overruled on the grounds of economy," said the directors' report on the affairs of the Victoria Market Company. A fish stall, a meat stall and a fruit stall had been rented at $10 per month. Farmers who did not wish to rent stalls could drive into the market yard from Broughton Street and sell produce from their cart for 50 cents a day.

The company had high expectations that the farmers' market and the weekly auctions of livestock and hay would prove successful. But this was not to be, for no sooner had the market opened than rumours began to circulate that the Victoria Market Company was unstable, with insufficient capital to maintain it. Some investors withdrew, others defaulted and in mid November, only two months after the market opened, the company declared bankruptcy and its assets were auctioned off to meet their liabilities. On October 20, 1861, the *Victoria Press* reported confirmation of the rumour that "a well-known member of the Assembly has offered $800 for the building" when John Cochrane obtained the property for $750.

Speculation began as to the future of the building. Some thought it would be converted into barracks for a "mythical" regiment of soldiers that had been promised by the British government. Others suggested it would make a fine lunatic asylum for the shareholders. Instead, it became a dance house, and the subject of many complaints, like this one expressed in the *Victoria Press* on December 22, 1861: "It is painful to see the new market building which has been erected with a very laudable object – that of improving the city – turned into a receptacle for Harlotry and all the worst vices of human nature."

The lots and the buildings passed through a number of hands over the next decade. In 1878, grocer James Fell bought the lot at the southeast corner of Fort and Broad streets and demolished the building that had been part of the 1861 market (see page 25). Fell continued to sell groceries on Broad Street as he had since coming to Victoria in 1859.

At least part of the reason for the failure of the market was the difficulty that farmers faced when they tried to bring their goods into town along the notoriously bad roads. "A farmer might as well endeavour to get his produce to one of the fixed stars as to bring it to market in Victoria," said one resident in a letter to the editor of the *Victoria Press* on

Road up to W. Pierce's Home, Fernwood,
October 1861. Barbara Lindley Crease
watercolour; BC Archives PDP01407.

December 2, 1861. At that time there were relatively few farmers in the area, and the amount of produce they could bring to town was limited. Perhaps, in spite of their stated need for a market, the farmers found it was easier, after all, to sell directly to grocers and households.

The failure of the market did not stop the citizens from expressing a desire for such a convenience, even though they had not supported it when it was available. J.P. Davies, who owned an auction house on Wharf Street, acquired some of the land on Fort Street in 1866 and established Davies' Cattle Market. The Colonist (December 21, 1866) described it as "quite an extensive affair [with] commodious sheds and stables where cattle and sheep were auctioned regularly". Davies claimed that the yard was unsurpassed on the Pacific Coast. He and the city reached agreement that a public market would be held two days a week for the next 10 years and that he would pay 25 per cent of the proceeds from rents and auction sales to the city.

The cattle-yard-cum-market provided an outlet for farmers, but the public continued to call for larger facilities. When the civic government proposed to build a new city hall in 1877, the public declared that a market was more important than an administrative building. The city agreed to establish a public market next to the city hall. It built some sheds at the back of the hall to serve as the market. But the *Colonist* called them "pigeon holes", without windows or awnings. "Costing two or three hundred dollars," said a *Colonist* editorial (June 1, 1879), they "seem intended for water closets, for which they seem admirably adapted". The city received no applications for them, so eventually used them as coal sheds and later removed them.

In 1881 and 1886 Victoria rate payers voted against bylaws to borrow money for the building of a new market. Finally, in 1890, they voted in favour, and once again watched as elaborate plans for the Victoria Public Market unfolded. The city purchased a site on the corner of Cormorant and Fisgard streets

Part of Victoria's Chinatown in 1886: the area that was burned down to make way for the market. Edouard Gaston Deville photograph; BC Archives D-04747.

for $42,000; it consisted of 3½ lots on Cormorant (now Pandora) Street and 5 lots on Fisgard. It hired John Teague, one of the most prominent architects in town, to design the structure for a fee of $2,537. The city received approval to borrow $100,000 for the market site and building. The future of the market seemed secure and the Bank of British North America advanced $35,200.

One hurdle remained. The site was in the middle of the Chinese section of town, filled with brick and wooden stores and dwellings. The best way to clear the site became a topic for discussion, as described in the *Colonist* on March 3, 1891:

> To Move or Burn: The question whether it would be better to remove or burn the old, tumbledown buildings on the market site is now puzzling the Market Committee. They are afraid if the buildings are sold a new Chinatown will be established in some other section of the city and this they wish to avoid. It is, therefore, probable that the outside buildings will be torn down and a grand bonfire made of the rest.

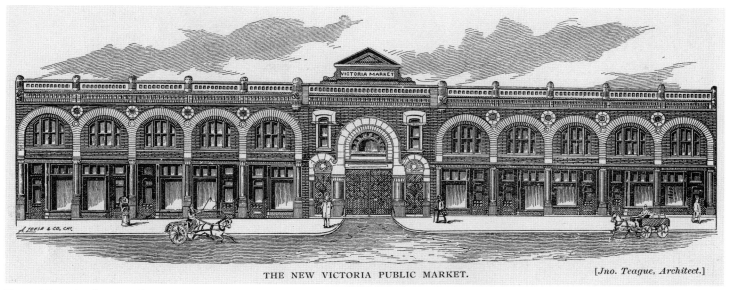

THE NEW VICTORIA PUBLIC MARKET.   [*Jno. Teague, Architect.*]

From *Victoria Illustrated*, 1891.

The decision was to burn. Years later, Victoria resident Frank Kelly reminisced about that night: "I remember the time the shacks which occupied the site of the market were put to the torch. It was quite a sizeable spectacle, particularly at night, when the Tiger and Deluge Company kept flames from spreading across the neighbourhood." Some spectators, in their excitement, got too close to the action – one man fell into a deep cesspool and had to be rescued. With the site cleared, the building could begin. The progress of the construction was followed with as much enthusiasm as it had been in 1861, and the promise it held for the community appeared as great.

The city awarded the building contract to McGregor & Jeeves, who carried out the construction for a total cost of $55,000. According to the *Colonist*, the new brick building surpassed all others in the city. A Nelson-granite archway formed the entrance, broad and high to accommodate horse-drawn vehicles. A roof of cathedral glass gave light to the interior (though on November 24, 1957, one observer

wrote to the *Colonist*, remembering the market as a "chill, gloomy building"). Iron beams and wooden pillars supported a gallery and the first floor. The iron beams were hollow and contained drain pipes, a new concept in sewage removal. Broad stairs led from the first floor up to the gallery. A circular bandstand jutted out from the gallery. Twelve electric lights hung from the ceiling and two ornamental fountains graced the ends of the building.

The spacious market accommodated all types of vendors. Six stores with large plate-glass windows faced outside on Cormorant Street. Behind them, six open shops faced into the market and more all around the building. Altogether the market held 60 stalls and stores, with rents ranging from $7.50 to $60 per month.

Unlike the financially cautious opening of the 1861 market, this new one opened with great fanfare on December 19, 1891. The Ladies Auxiliary of the Royal Jubilee Hospital organized the event, with the proceeds from ticket sales going to the BC Benevolent

Victoria Public Market by Susan Gibson. BC Archives PDP 04202.

Society, and they were more than pleasantly surprised when nearly 2000 people came. Evergreen swags decorated the gallery railings and Japanese lanterns hung everywhere. Red banners hung at each end of the market above the gallery, one with large, white wool letters saying "God Save the Queen" and the other "Welcome to the Victoria Market". A group called the Amateur Orchestra performed on toy instruments; others sang popular songs and recited poems and literary excerpts. Formal opening speeches followed, and then the dancing began. The band played in the gallery and dancing went on until midnight. The opening was considered a great success.

Despite this grand opening, the Victoria Public Market struggled to maintain its viability. During its first nine years the market never rented more than half its stalls, and many of the renters were not what one would expect to find in a farmer's market. The city rented to anyone who needed space, which resulted in a mixed use. A city hotel even rented some stalls to display samples of its rooms. The Salvation Army used one of the rooms for band and singing practice, and two militia groups used the centre of the hall as a drill hall. In 1897 a newcomer to the city expressed her puzzlement (quoted in a *Colonist* retrospective article, April 20, 1975), after she went to the market "to get some fresh eggs and some vegetables". She found that "the farmers were not in evidence.… I found a worn out fire engine or two, which I had no use for, a portrait painter's studio, a real estate agent, the Sanitary Inspector, and the most ghastly of all things – the public morgue was an annex of the market."

By 1899, the Victoria Fire Department had taken over the eastern half of the market building. There was some discussion in the newspapers about sharing the costs of the building equally. Some writers pointed out that while the fire department occupied a large portion of the building, its rent did not reflect

Victoria City Hall, 1897.
BC Archives H-02717.

this. In 1901, with business still low, the city rented the western part of the building to the Victoria and Sidney Railway as a freight and passenger station. This proved to be unsuitable, because the trains were not able to pull up the steep grade on Fisgard, and after just five years the station moved to Johnson and Store streets.

As the Victoria Public Market carried out less and less market business it became undeserving of the name. But the First World War gave it a temporary respite. Food supplies were desperately needed and tents were set up just west of the city hall to serve as a market. When the BC Electric Railway began picking up produce in Saanich on market days and delivering it to Victoria, the market thrived in the old building. But at the end of the war the decline began again.

Over the years the city made many improvements to the building in an effort to make the market more attractive to the vendors and the public. It replaced the original floor, repaired the glass roof following a heavy snow storm in 1916, increased the lighting, and finally installed glass doors to replace the old iron gates and to seal the market from the cold drafts. Each improvement resulted in an increase in fees, until the market was no longer sustainable. It continued to struggle through the 1950s and finally closed in 1959 when it was demolished

The Victoria Fire Department at the east end of the Victoria Public Market building, 1890s. The main entrance to the market is just to the right of the awning. BC Archives G-04713.

Victoria Public Market in 1959, just before being demolished.
BC Archives B-09363.

Chinese vegetable peddler on Fish Road, Gordon Head, 1908. Delivery to the door was more convenient than a trip to the public market in town. BC Archives E-02063.

and the development of Market Square began. Nine stall owners banded together and operated a small farmers market at 618 Pandora Street in an effort to keep the tradition alive.

Many reasons can be found for the inability of the city to sustain the market that everybody said they wanted even more than a new city hall. The reasons differed as years went by, but the basic problem appeared to be a lack of support from both farmers and customers. Transporting produce to the market was difficult, and the market offered no delivery service at a time when the average family had no readily available transportation other than walking or the tram. When cars became more common, there was little parking space near the market. Chinese farmers continued to deliver fresh vegetables to people's homes; horse-drawn wagons replaced their yoked baskets and then trucks replaced the wagons.

Farmers continued delivering their fruit and vegetables door to door just as they had for decades. Small neighbourhood groceries abounded, featuring home-grown fruit and vegetables. Precursors of the supermarkets began to appear in the 1920s, and by the end of the decade the chain supermarkets, such as Piggly Wiggly and Safeway, had established stores in convenient locations offering a wide range of goods. These large stores brought in the modern era of supplying food and drink to the citizens of Victoria and British Columbia.

Ad in the *Colonist* on November 25, 1928, urging shoppers to buy products made in British Columbia.

Appendix
Colourful Labels and Containers

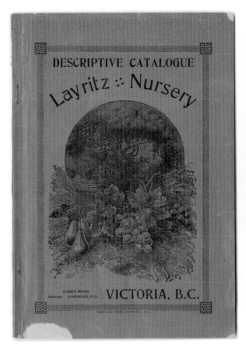

978.51.3.

965.2213.1.

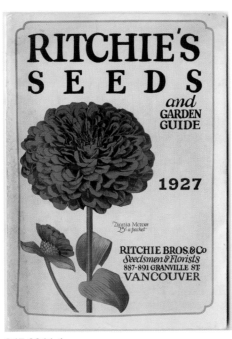

965.2211.1a.

One of the earliest nurserymen in Victoria was Jonathan Begg in 1860, but over time Layritz Nurseries seemed to represent Victoria's enthusiasm for gardening. After an initial failure in 1887, Richard Layritz established a successful nursery in 1900 – and it flourished for more than 50 years. Layritz gained an international reputation, but still faced competition from Vancouver suppliers like the Ritchie Brothers and from even farther afield by prominent Toronto supplier William Rennie Company.

All items shown in the appendix reside in the history collection of the Royal BC Museum.

Box label, 990.52.3e.

Window decal, 972.258.2.

Biscuits came in tins and boxes and, later, paper packages.

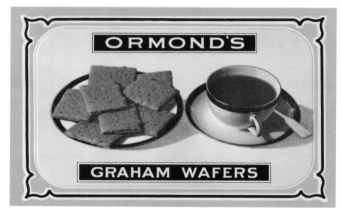

Box label, 990.52.3d.

Tin box, 990.53.3e.

Box label, 990.52.3o.

Tin pail, 997.50.37a-b.

Syphons (left to right) Old English 967.37.2; Morley 967.37.3; Kirk & Co. 965.431.2; Duncan 2009.93.1.

971.211.8a.

Ramsay's biscuit tin, Victoria, 987.7.499.

985.79.13.

2000.33.35.

2000.48.27.

990.52.3b.

990.52.3g.

Eaton's tea tin, 987.7.386.

987.41.4.

987.7.462.

971.61.1584.

987.7.376.

972.263.26.

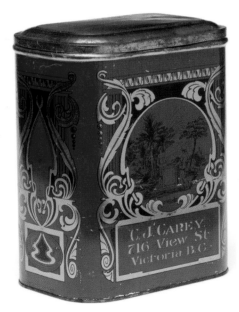

2006.14.2.

971.253.45.

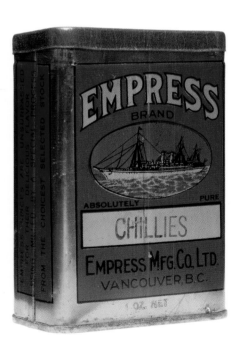

976.81.10f.

987.7.513.

990.59.1a-b.

987.7.507.

990.59.3.

976.81.22.

979.107.2a.

989.23.215.

989.23.150.

989.23.393.

979.107.2a.

Facing page: Local and imported brands of spices:
Jameson's of Victoria; Nabob, Malkin and Spencer's
of Vancouver; and Red & White with branches across
Canada, including Vancouver.

989.23.362.

989.23.380.

989.23.382.

989.23.323.

990.52.3p.

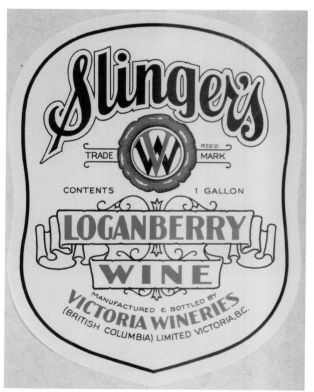

990.52.3q.

990.52.3m.

990.52.3j.

990.52.3h.

990.52.3f.

Grower's Winery opened in Victoria in 1922; its
first product was Logana wine (above), made from
loganberries. Victoria Wineries opened in 1927; its main
brand was Slinger's loganberry wine (facing page). In 1932
Victoria Wineries merged with Grower's.

990.52.3k.

990.52.3l.

990.52.3v.

990.52.3u.

990.52.3l.

990.52.3i.

Two can labels (above)
and a box label.

964.80.1.

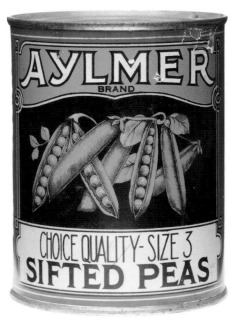

971.77.13.

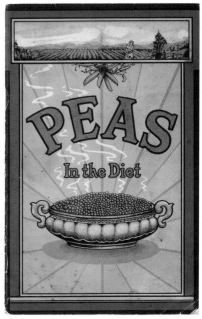

Brochure from Broder Canning,
New Westminster. 971.77.13.

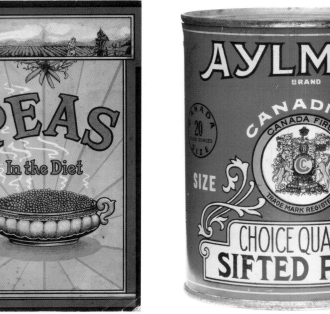

987.41.2.

987.7.403.

987.7.393, front and back.

987.7.395, front and back.

Baking Powder packed in Victoria.
987.7.437.

984.80.1.

990.52.3s.

990.52.3n.

Bulmans of Vernon began producing dehydrated fruit in 1916 and began canning about 1928. One their main products was tomato ketchup. 2000.33.61.

Front (left) and back of a granulated potato tin can re-used to hold tea. 982.134 115.

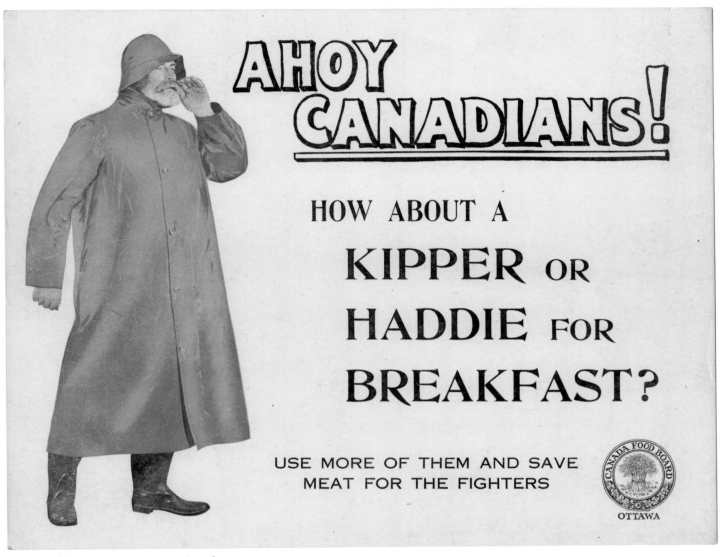

First World War poster promoting the
civilian consumption of fish rather
than meat. 976.58.15b.

Colourful invoices from various retailers to Judge Peter O'Reilly and Dr John Helmcken.

Acknowledgements

As every author knows, very few books are written without considerable help from many individuals and this is often especially true for history books.

In this case we would like to particularly thank Gerry Truscott, who spent countless hours editing and preparing the book for printing. We would also like to express our appreciation to Greg Evans for his contribution of the chapter on local brewing.

There are many others who helped us. Thank you to the BC Archives staff whose patience always makes the search for images easier, to Kim Martin and Carlo Mocellin for their wonderful photographs of artifacts shown in this book, and to Delphine Castles for getting the objects safely to the studio and back to the RBCM's history collection.

Thanks also to Carrie Palliser at the City of Victoria Archives; Peter Garnham at the Sidney Archives for information about Brackman & Ker; Dave Parker, formerly with the Esquimalt Archives; and Dave Minaker. Sister Margaret Cantwell (SSA) gave us information about the farming ventures of the Sisters of St Ann. Conversations with other researchers, including Chris Hanna and Sharon Keen, helped us shape ideas and pointed us to new information.

Nancy Oke and Bob Griffin

Feeding the Family

Edited by Gerry Truscott (RBCM) and Robert Moyes.

Pages designed and produced by Gerry Truscott; set in Palatino Linotype (11/13 body, 10/12 captions).

Cover designed and typeset by Chris Tyrrell and Michael Carter, RBCM.

Digital photographic production by Kelly-Ann Turkington, Kim Martin, Carlo Mocellin and Gerry Truscott, RBCM.

Archival photographs, paintings and drawings in black and white from BC Archives, except where noted in the caption. Artifact photographs in colour or black and white by Kim Martin and Carlo Mocellin, RBCM, except where noted in the caption. All images not belonging to the Royal BC Museum have been reprinted with permission.

Printed by Kromar Printing, Winnipeg.

About the Authors

Nancy Oke has been a research volunteer at the Royal BC Museum for several years. When she began examining artifacts related to food packaging in the collection, she became interested in the people who supplied these groceries in early Victoria. This research inspired her to write *Feeding the Family*.

Dr Robert Griffin has been a history curator at the Royal BC Museum for 30 years and now manages the History section. He has written many articles on the industrial history of the province, and has curated several museum exhibitions.

Greg Evans wrote his MA thesis on the history of beer brewing in Victoria and has since written many popular articles on the subject. He is the municipal archivist for the Township of Esquimalt.

About the Royal BC Museum

British Columbia is a big land with a unique history. As the province's museum and archives, the Royal BC Museum captures British Columbia's story and shares it with the world. It does so by collecting, preserving and interpreting millions of artifacts, specimens and documents of provincial significance, and by producing publications, exhibitions and public programs that bring the past to life in exciting, innovative and personal ways. The Royal BC Museum helps to explain what it means to be British Columbian and to define the role this province plays in the world.

The Royal BC Museum administers a unique cultural precinct in the heart of BC's capital city. This site incorporates the Royal BC Museum (est. 1886), the BC Archives (est. 1894), the Netherlands Centennial Carillon, Helmcken House, St Ann's Schoolhouse and Thunderbird Park, which is home to Wawaditła (Mungo Martin House).

Although its buildings are located in Victoria, the Royal BC Museum has a mandate to serve all citizens of the province, wherever they live. It meets this mandate by: conducting and supporting field research; lending artifacts, specimens and documents to other institutions; publishing books (like this one) about BC's history and environment; producing travelling exhibitions; delivering a variety of services by phone, fax, mail and e-mail; and providing a vast array of information on its website about all of its collections and holdings.

From its inception 125 years ago, the Royal BC Museum has been led by people who care passionately about this province and work to fulfil its mission to preserve and share the story of British Columbia.

Find out more about the Royal BC Museum at www.royalbcmuseum.bc.ca

Bibliography

Newspapers, especially the *Colonist*, provided most of the information for this book. This bibliography lists newspapers first, then directories and merchant records, and finally other sources.

Newspapers

All of these newspapers operated in Victoria, except for the *San Francisco Daily Evening Bulletin*. "*Vancouver*" in some newspaper names refers to Vancouver Island. The dates listed are those covered in this book, though for many (e.g., the *Colonist*) they also measure the entire run of the paper.

Colonist, published over the years under the following names:
> *British Colonist, The.* 1858 – July 28, 1860.
> *Daily British Colonist, The.* July 31, 1860 – August 6, 1872.
> *Daily British Colonist.* August 7, 1872 – December 31, 1886.
> *The Daily Colonist.* January 1, 1887 – 1946.

Courrier de la Nouvelle Caledonie, Le. September 11 – October 8, 1858.
Daily Evening Express. April 27, 1863 – June 30, 1864.
Daily Victoria Gazette. July 28 – October 26, 1858.
Industrial News. December 26, 1885 – December 18, 1886.
San Francisco Daily Evening Bulletin. June 23, 1858.
Vancouver Daily Post. August 11–14, 1865.
Vancouver Daily Evening Post. September 8, 1865 – April 29, 1866.
Vancouver Island Gazette. July 28 – August 9, 1858.
Vancouver Times. September 5, 1864 – March 31, 1865.
Vancouver Times and Evening Express. April 9–10, 1865.
Victoria Daily Chronicle. October 28, 1862 – June 23, 1866.
Victoria Daily Standard, The. June 20, 1870 – August 4, 1888.
Victoria Gazette. June 25 – July 24, 1858, October 28 – November 26, 1858.
Victoria Gazette, for circulation in California, the Atlantic States and Europe. August 4 – September 2, 1858.
Victoria Weekly Gazette. August 4 – September 29, 1860.
Weekly Victoria Gazette. August 14, 1858 – November 26, 1859.

Merchant Accounts, Daybooks and Journals

Carr, Richard. 1836–81. Diary and accounts. BC Archives MS-0610.
Calder family. 1869–1925. Account books. BC Archives MS-2615.
Dawley, Walter Thomas. 1894-1969. Accounts and invoices. BC Archives MS-1076.
Grocery store. 1885–89. Daybooks. BC Archives MS-1958.
Grocery store. 1886–87. Daybook. BC Archives MS-2710.
Harrison, William. 1882–1911. Account books. BC Archives MS-0795.
Menagerie and museum. 1857–82. Account book. BC Archives MS-2082.

Merchant. 1866–69. Ledger. BC Archives MS-2645.

Merchant. 1867–70. Ledger. BC Archives MS-0076.

Murray, Ninian C. 1865–70. Ledger. BC Archives MS-2687.

O'Sullivan, Humphrey. 1862–90. Accounts. BC Archives MS-2607.

Stewart, John Robertson. 1863–70. Commission Agent, Victoria: bills and invoices. BC Archives MS-2579.

Thoburn Grocery, Esquimalt. 1909–26. Account books. BC Archives MS-1185.

Directories

British Columbia Directory, The. 1882–83, 1884–85, 1889, 1890, 1891, 1892, 1895, 1899.

British Columbia Directory. 1925, 1930.

British Columbia Gazetteer and Directory. 1905, 1908, 1912, 1920.

British Columbian and Victoria Guide, The. 1863.

First Victoria Directory. 1860, 1868, 1869.

Greater Victoria Directory. 1933–34.

Guide to the Province of British Columbia. 1877–78.

Victoria Directory. 1874.

Other Sources

Adams, Emma H. 1898. *To and fro, up and down in Southern California, Oregon, and Washington Territory, with sketches in Arizona, New Mexico, and British Columbia.* San Francisco: Hunt & Eaton.

Anderson, James. nd. "Notes and comments on early days and events in British Columbia, Washington and Oregon including an account of sundry happenings in San Francisco; being the memoirs of James Robert Anderson written by himself." BC Archives MS-1912, Box 9.

Bagshaw, Roberta L. ed. 1996. *No Better Land: The 1860 Diaries of the Anglican Colonial Bishop George Hills.* Victoria: Sono Nis Press.

Baskerville, Peter A. 1986. *Beyond the Island: A Visual History of Victoria.* Burlington: Windsor Publications.

Bayley, Charles Alfred. 1830-1889. "Early Life on Vancouver Island." BC Archives E/B/B34.2.

Beeman, Samuel O. 1864–69. Letters. BC Archives MS-2073, microfilm, A01401.

Beeton, Isabella. 1880. *The Book of Household Management.* London: Ward, Lock & Co.

Begg, Alexander. 1894. *History of British Columbia from its Earliest Discovery to the Present Time.* Toronto: W. Briggs.

Bell, Betty. 1982. *The Fair Land.* Victoria: Sono Nis Press.

Blake, Anson S. 1949. "Hudson's Bay Company in San Francisco." *California Historical Society Quarterly*, vol. 28.

Blakey Smith, Dorothy, ed. 1975. *The Reminiscences of Doctor John Sebastian Helmcken.* Vancouver: University of British Columbia Press.

Bowsfield, Hartwell, ed. 1979. *Fort Victoria Letters 1846–1851.* Hudson's Bay Record Society, vol. 32.

British Columbia, Colony of. 1859–69. Customs House Returns. BC Archives GR-2957.

Brotchie, William. 1843, 1858. Bill of lading and a receipt. BC Archives MS-612.

Bulkley, Thomas A. 1872. Victoria Water Supply. Report. BC Archives NWp 971.93 B934.

Burns, Robert J. 1985. *Packaging Food and Other Consumer Goods in Canada, 1867–1927: A Guide to Federal Specifications for Bulk and Unit Containers, Their Labels and Contents.* Ottawa: Parks Canada.

Careless, J.M.S. 1972. "The Business Community in the Early Development of Victoria, British Columbia." *Canadian Business History: Selected Studies 1497–1971.* Toronto: McClelland and Stewart.

Carr, Emily. 1942. *The Book of Small.* Toronto: Irwin Publishing.

Cauthers, Janet, ed. 1978. "A Victoria Tapestry: Impressions of Life in Victoria, BC, 1880–1914". *Sound Heritage*, vol. 7.

Crease, Sarah. 1860. Memo book. BC Archives A/E/C86/C861.3 and A/E/C86/C861.6.

Crease, Susan R. 1948. Personal reflections. BC Archives A/E/C86/C864.1

Daily Colonist, The. 1891. *Victoria Illustrated.* Victoria: The Daily Colonist.

Dairy plants. 1929. Tickets and receipts. BC Archives MS-0241.

Davies, Bill. 1990. *From Sourdough to Superstore: History of Kelly Douglas*. Vancouver: Kelly Douglas.

Dawley, Walter Thomas. 1894–1969. Accounts and invoices. BC Archives MS-1076.

Edgar and Aimé. 1860–62. Correspondence book. BC Archives MS-2595.

Evans, Charles. 1835(?)–71. Diary. BC Archives MS-0308.

Fawcett, Edgar. 1912. *Some Reminiscences of Old Victoria*. Toronto: William Briggs.

Fawcett family. 1864–1916. Reminiscences. BC Archives MS-1962, Box 2.

Floyd, Patrick Donald. 1969. "The Human Geography of Southeastern Vancouver Island". MA thesis, University of Victoria.

Fort Victoria. 1844–61. Records. Hudson's Bay Company. BC Archives A/B/20/Vi3F, A/C/15/H86, A/C/20/Vi, A/D/20/S2T/J, A/D/20/Vi9.

———. 1844–58. Correspondence books and post journal. Hudson's Bay Company Archives 1M149, microfilms B226/b/1-5; 1M233, microfilms B.226/b/48; and 1M149, microfilm B226/a/1.

Frawley, Carol Mavis. 1971. "Continuity and Change: The Role of the Hudson's Bay Company in Oregon and Vancouver Island, 1824–1859." MA thesis, University of Victoria.

Gosnell, R.E. 1897. *The Year Book of British Columbia and Manual of Provincial Information*. Victoria: King's Printer.

Government House. 1877. Records. BC Archives GR-0868, B1092, File 20 2298.

Greene, R.A. 1961. "The Fernwood Bakery" and "Corner Grocery". *Transactions of the Canadian Numismatic Research Society*, vol. 4, issue 2.

Gregson, Harry. 1970. *A History of Victoria: 1842–1970*. Victoria: Victoria Observer Publishing.

Harris, Martha. 1896–1901. Correspondence, BC Archives MS-2789, Box 1.

Helmcken, Anslie J. 1967. "Main Street Victoria, 1908." *Colonist*, March 5.

Hendrickson, James, ed. 1980. *Journals of the Colonial Legislature of the Colonies of Vancouver Island and British Columbia, 1851–1871*, vol. 3: *Journals of the House of Assembly, Vancouver Island, 1863–1866*. Victoria: Provincial Archives of British Columbia.

Hudson's Bay Company. 1850–71. Correspondence outward. Hudson's Bay Company. BC Archives A/C/15.

International Tin Research and Development Council. 1939. *Historic Tinned Foods*. Greenford: International Tin Research and Development Council.

Ireland, W.E. 1941. "Early Flour Mills in British Columbia, Part 1". *British Columbia Historical Quarterly*, vol. 2 (April).

———. 1948. "Gold-Rush Days in Victoria, 1858–1859". *British Columbia Historical Quarterly*, vol. 12 (July).

Kelly, Frank. 1950. "The Public Market". *Colonist*, August 5.

———. 1957. "Reminiscences". *Colonist*, August 5.

Kluckner, Michael. 1986. *Victoria: The Way It Was*. North Vancouver: Whitecap Books.

Labouchere, Henry. 1849–57. Correspondence. BC Archives MS-0310.

Lai, David Chuenyan. 1988. *Chinatowns: Towns Within Cities in Canada*. Vancouver: UBC Press.

Laing, F.W. 1941. "Early Flour Mills in British Columbia, Part 2". *British Columbia Historical Quarterly*, vol. 3 (July).

Lamb, W. Kaye. 1943. "The Diary of Robert Melrose". *British Columbia Historical Quarterly*, April, July, October.

MacDonald, William John. 1914. "A Pioneer, 1851". BC Archives NWp 971K M135.

MacFie, Matthew. 1865. *Vancouver Island and British Columbia*. London: publisher unknown.

Mackie, R.S. 1984. "Colonial Land, Indian Labour and Company Capital: the Economy of Vancouver Island 1849–1858." MA thesis, University of Victoria. BC Archives MS-2060.

MacMillan, Alexander. 1891–1911. Diaries. BC Archives MS-073, microfilm A00951.

McKenzie family. 1852–73. Papers relating to Craigflower Farm. BC Archives MS-2431, microfilms A01392-1395 and A01492-1493.

McTavish, George Simpson. 1963. *Behind the Palisades: An Autobiography of George Simpson McTavish*. Victoria: E. Gurd.

Moody, Mary Susanna. 1858–63. Correspondence. BC Archives MS-1101.

Nesbitt, James K. 1952. "Old Houses and Families". *Colonist*, July 6.

Newcombe family. 1912–24. Accounts. BC Archives MS-1077, vol. 233, files 3, 4.

O'Reilly family. 1830–1960. Household accounts. BC Archives MS-2894.

———. 1856–1963. Records. BC Archives MS-0412.

Pethick, Derek. 1968. *Victoria: The Fort*. Vancouver: Mitchell Press.

———. 1969. *James Douglas: Servant of Two Empires*. Vancouver: Mitchell Press.

———. 1980. *Summer of Promise: Victoria 1864–1914*. Victoria: Sono Nis Press.

Pidcock. Reginald Heber. 1862. "Adventures in Vancouver Island". BC Archives MS-0728, Box 2.

Rithet, Robert P. 1868. Rithet family papers. BC Archives MS-504.

Robertson, Irene Elaine. 1982. "The Business Community and the Development of Victoria, 1858–1900." MA thesis, University of Victoria.

Shepard, M.P., and A.W. Argue. 1989. *The Commercial Harvest of Salmon in British Columbia, 1820–1977*. Vancouver: Department of Fisheries and Oceans.

Sivertz, Gus. 1956. "When We Were Very Young". *Victoria Times*, January 15.

Spencer Ltd, David. 1937. Mail Order Quality Food Specials. BC Archives.

Spoehr, Alexander. 1986. "Fur Traders in Hawaii: The Hudson's Bay Company in Honolulu, 1829–1861". *Hawaiian Journal of History*, vol. 20.

———. 1988. "A 19th Century Chapter in Hawaii's Maritime History: Hudson's Bay Company Merchant Shipping, 1829–1859". *Hawaii Journal of History*, vol. 22.

Vancouver Island Treasury. Trade Licenses Assessment Rolls. BC Archives C/AA/30.26.

Victoria Market Company. 1861. "Opening of New Market" (broadside). BC Archives NWp 971.95Vi V645m.

———. 1861. "Report on the Affairs of the Victoria Market Company, Limited." BC Archives NWp 971.95Vi V645mr.

Victoria Water Supply. 1946. BC Archives NWp971.83 V642.

Victoria, City of. Annual reports. 1882–1941. City of Victoria Archives.

———. By-laws. 1877–1931. City of Victoria Archives.

Waddington, Alfred. 1858. *The Fraser Mines Vindicated*. Vancouver: Robert Reid.

Watson, Robert. 1930. "The Hudson's Bay Company in the Hawaiian Islands." *The Beaver*, vol. 10.

Williams, R.T. 1894–98. Scrapbook. BC Archives MS-2613.

Wilson, Bill, and Jim Askey. 1986. *Pioneer Soda Water Companies of BC*. New Westminster: Tamahi Publishing.

Wolfenden, Richard. 1900–1903. Invoices. BC Archives MS-2581.

Index